FIT FÜR DIE SCHULE

Englisch trainieren

Basiswissen

Von Werner Zenker
Illustrationen von Marcus Frey
Coverillustration
von Manfred Tophoven

TESSLOFF

Liebe Schülerin, lieber Schüler,

mit diesem Heft hast du die Möglichkeit, den grundlegenden Grammatikstoff der englischen Sprache zu wiederholen und zu üben.

Das Übungsheft ist in verschiedene Kapitel gegliedert, die den wichtigsten Lernstoff der ersten Englischjahre beinhalten. Der Lernstoff wird erklärt und durch vielfältige Übungen gefestigt.

Du kannst die einzelnen Kapitel der Reihe nach bearbeiten. Wenn du ganz gezielt ein bestimmtes Thema üben möchtest, kannst du es mit dem Inhaltsverzeichnis finden, den Lernstoff wiederholen und dann die dazugehörigen Aufgaben bearbeiten.

Im Anschluss an den Aufgabenteil findest du die Lösungen zu den einzelnen Aufgaben. Aber bitte erst nachschauen, wenn du die entsprechende Aufgabe gelöst hast! Eine Liste mit unregelmäßigen Verben und eine Vokabelliste schließen sich an den Lösungsteil an.

Viel Erfolg!

Werner Zenker

Inhalt

Die Zahlen

Dies sind die Zahlen von 1 bis 9 in Englisch:

one two three four five six seven eight nine

1 Wenn man jemandem seine Telefonnummer sagt, nennt man die einzelnen Ziffern nacheinander. Schreibe die folgenden Telefonnummern auf, wie im Beispiel.

9 4 7 8 3	nine	four	seven	eight	three
5 1 6 2 4	______	______	______	______	______
2 4 9 8 6	______	______	______	______	______
3 1 5 6 8	______	______	______	______	______
4 2 8 5 9	______	______	______	______	______

2 Hier kommt noch die Null dazu. Wenn man jemandem die Telefonnummer nennt, wird die Null wie das englische “o” ausgesprochen. Schreibe auch diese Telefonnummern auf.

4 0 5 0 3 2	four	o	five	o	three	two
6 0 0 9 7 3	______	______	______	______	______	______
1 9 0 6 8 9	______	______	______	______	______	______
3 0 8 0 7 5	______	______	______	______	______	______
8 5 9 8 0 2	______	______	______	______	______	______

3 Welche Telefonnummern werden hier genannt? Kreuze die beiden richtigen Nummern an!

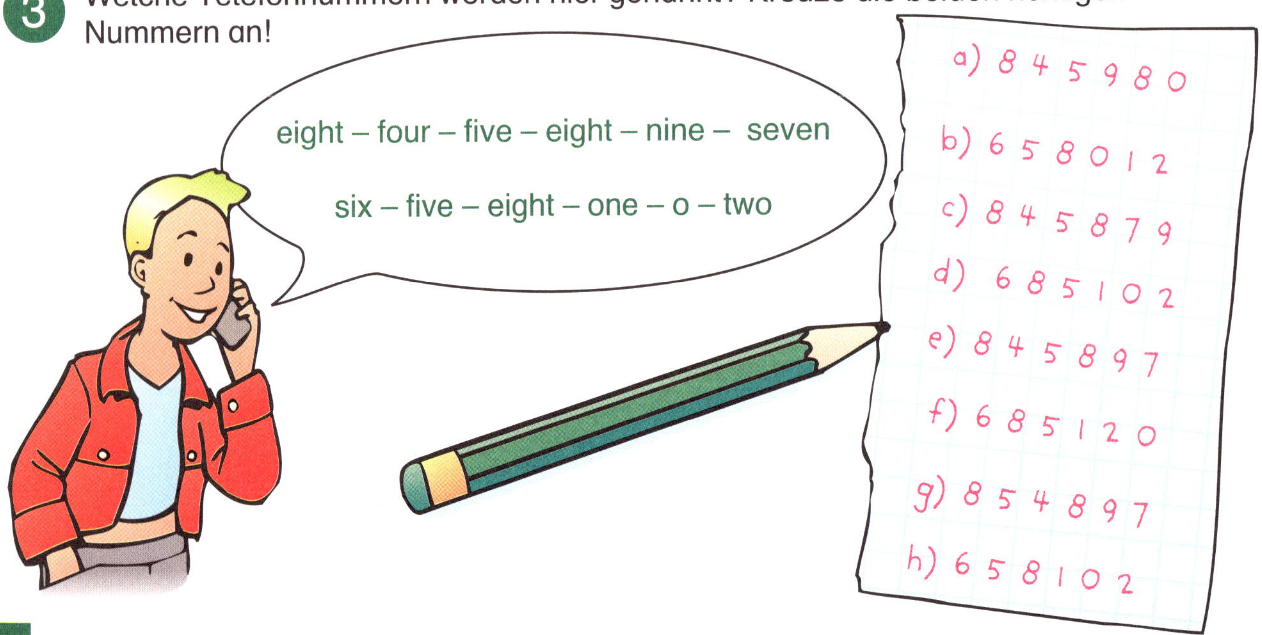

Die Zahlen 10, 11 und 12 haben eigene Namen.

10 ten
11 eleven
12 twelve

Die Zahlen von 13 – 19 setzen sich aus der Einerzahl und der Endung "-teen" zusammen. Aber aufgepasst! Es gibt Abweichungen beim Schreiben! Merk dir die Schreibweise der grün geschriebenen Wörter besonders gut.

13 thirteen	17 seventeen
14 fourteen	18 eighteen
15 fifteen	19 nineteen
16 sixteen	

Die Zehnerzahlen ab 20 haben alle die Endung "-ty". Auch hier kann man sich nicht immer darauf verlassen, dass sie am Anfang so geschrieben werden wie der entsprechende Einer. Achte deshalb auch hier besonders auf die Schreibweise der grün geschriebenen Wörter.

20 twenty	60 sixty
30 thirty	70 seventy
40 forty	80 eighty
50 fifty	90 ninety

100 heißt "one hundred" oder "a hundred".

100 one hundred / a hundred

1 Alle anderen Zahlen setzt man zusammen, indem zuerst der Zehner und dann der Einer genannt wird. Beim Schreiben werden sie mit einem Bindestrich verbunden. Schreibe jeweils die entsprechenden Zahlen vor die Wörter.

49	forty-nine	____	thirty-one	____	sixty-three	____	twenty-four
____	eighty-four	____	sixty-six	____	fifty-nine	____	seventy-eight

2 Schreibe jeweils neben die Personen, wie alt sie sind.

5 ____________

12 ____________

27 ____________

48 ____________

55 ____________

100 ____________

Die Uhrzeit

So werden im Englischen die vollen Stunden genannt:

3.00	7.00	9.00
three o'clock	seven o'clock	nine o'clock

1 Schreibe unter diese Uhren, wie spät es ist.

6.00	4.00	12.00
a) six o'clock	b) ______	c) ______
1.00	11.00	2.00
d) ______	e) ______	f) ______

2 Wenn man die Uhrzeit von einer Digitaluhr abliest, werden im Englischen nur die Zahlen genannt – zuerst die Stunden, dann die Minuten. Die Null wird "o" genannt.

1.18	4.49	10.07	2.35	aber:	5.00
one eighteen	four forty-nine	ten o seven	two thirty-five		five o'clock

Schreibe die Uhrzeiten auf.

a) 6.19 ______
b) 5.07 ______
c) 10.39 ______
d) 0.41 ______
e) 3.58 ______
f) 7.00 ______
g) 11.32 ______
h) 8.13 ______
i) 2.21 ______
j) 12.00 ______
k) 4.07 ______

Beim Ablesen der Uhrzeit von der Zeigeruhr wird unterschieden, ob eine volle Stunde erst kurz vorbei ist oder ob sie kurz bevorsteht.

eight o'clock | five past eight | a quarter past eight | twenty-five past eight

half past eight | twenty-five to nine | twenty to nine | a quarter to nine | ten to nine

Anders als im Deutschen heißt „halb neun" im Englischen "half past eight". Das gilt natürlich auch für alle anderen halben Stunden!

1 Schreibe die Uhrzeiten unter die Zeigeruhr. Verwende immer "past" oder "to".

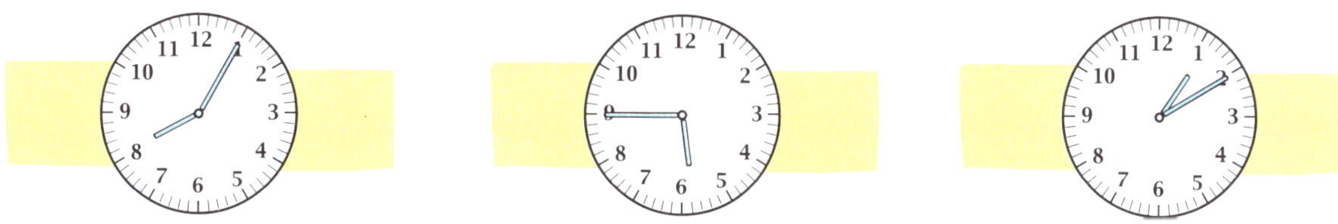

a) ______________ b) ______________ c) ______________

d) ______________ e) ______________ f) ______________

g) ______________ h) ______________ i) ______________

Ordnungszahlen

Bei den englischen Ordnungszahlen wird außer bei "first", "second" und "third" meist ein -th an die Zahl angehängt. Bei den Zehnerzahlen ändert sich dann die Schreibweise! Wenn man Ordnungszahlen nicht als Wort schreibt, sondern als Zahl, dann werden -st, -nd, -rd oder -th direkt an die Zahl angehängt.

1 Schau dir genau an, wie die Ordnungszahlen im Englischen gebildet werden. Schreibe sie als Zahl.

____ first	____ ninth	____ eighth	____ eleventh
____ thirty-second	____ forty-fourth	____ fiftieth	____ fifteenth
____ sixty-first	____ eighty-third	____ ninety-ninth	____ thirtieth

2 Bei der Hunde-Ausstellung hat jeder Hund einen Preis bekommen, auch der letzte. Welchen Rang der Hund erreicht hat, erkennst du an der Zahl in den Bildern. Schreibe die passende Ordnungszahl als englisches Wort dazu.

Dog´s Championship!

1st first
2nd second
3rd third
4th fourth
5th fifth
6th sixth
7th seventh
8th eighth
9th ninth
10th tenth
11th eleventh
12th twelfth
13th thirteenth
14th fourteenth
15th fifteenth
16th sixteenth
17th seventeenth
18th eighteenth
19th nineteenth
20th twentieth
21th twenty-first
22th twenty-second
23rd twenty-third
24rd twenty-fourth
25th twenty-fifth
26th twenty-sixth
27th twenty-seventh
28th twenty-eighth
29th twenty-ninth
30th thirtieth
31st thirty-first
32th thirty-second
33rd thirty-third
34th thirty-fourth
...

40th fortieth
41st forty-first
42nd forty-second
43rd forty-third
44th forty-fourth
...
50th fiftieth
51st fifty-first
52nd fifty-second
53rd fifty-third
54th fifty-fourth
...
60th sixtieth
61st sixty-first
62nd sixty-second
63rd sixty-third
64th sixty-fourth
...
70th seventieth
71st seventy-first
72nd seventy-second
73rd seventy-third
74th seventy-fourth
...
80th eightieth
81st eighty-first
82nd eighty-second
83rd eighty-third
84th eighty-fourth
...
90th ninetieth
91st ninety-first
92nd ninety-second
93rd ninety-third
94th ninety-fourth
...

Monate und Wochentage

Alle Monatsnamen werden im Englischen großgeschrieben. Hier stehen sie in der Reihenfolge des Jahresablaufs:

January..........February..........March..........April..........May..........June
July......August......September......October......November......December

1 Wie heißt der vierte Monat des Jahres? Und wie der siebte Monat? Und der zwölfte? Schreibe die entsprechenden Monatsnamen auf Englisch auf.

4th month: ______	7th month: ______
12th month: ______	9th month: ______
10th month: ______	5th month: ______
1st month: ______	8th month: ______
3rd month: ______	6th month: ______
11th month: ______	2nd month: ______

2 Die Wochentage werden im Englischen immer großgeschrieben. Wie sie heißen, siehst du an diesen Kalenderblättern aus verschiedenen Monaten:

Die richtige Reihenfolge der sieben Wochentage von Montag bis Sonntag kennst du. Schreibe sie hier in Englisch auf.

Mon ______ ______ ______ ______
______ ______ ______ = the week

3 Schau dir die Kalenderblätter in der oberen Reihe genau an. Dann weißt du, auf welchen Wochentag diese Tage gefallen sind. Schreibe sie in Englisch auf.

December	June	March	May	October
13	11	7	22	29
______	______	______	______	______

Namen und Nomen

Im Englischen werden genauso wie im Deutschen alle Namen von Personen großgeschrieben.

Laura | Chris | Susan | Mr Smith | Mrs Miller | Miss Clark

Die meisten anderen Nomen (Hauptwörter) werden kleingeschrieben – also anders als im Deutschen!

1 Hier siehst du jeweils eine Person zusammen mit einem Tier. Schreibe auf, wen du da siehst und welches Tier dabei ist, so wie im Beispiel.

a) Laura / mouse

b) ____________________

c) ____________________

d) ____________________

e) ____________________

f) ____________________

Außer Eigennamen, Monaten und Wochentagen werden im Englischen auch alle Ländernamen großgeschrieben:

D	F	E	DK	I
Germany	France	Spain	Denmark	Italy

Häufige Nomen

Hier findest du einige Nomen, die sehr häufig gebraucht werden.
Du solltest sie alle gut kennen.

schoolbag church pencil sun house
table lorry ship bed
rubber book
tower cupboard tree street moon
plane
bridge pen
river
bus bike chair car flower
boat pencil case star

1 Wie heißen die Dinge, neben denen auf diesem Bild ein Buchstabe steht? Schreibe die richtigen Wörter auf.

a) ____________ b) ____________ c) ____________
d) ____________ e) ____________ f) ____________
g) ____________ h) ____________ i) ____________
j) ____________ k) ____________ l) ____________

2 Welches Wort passt nicht zu den anderen? Streiche es durch.

a) bus – ship – flower – car
b) tower – house – church – pencil
c) rubber – pen – book – plane
d) sun – moon – star – bed
e) table – bed – river – cupboard

Bestimmte und unbestimmte Artikel

Vor den Nomen stehen auch im Englischen häufig Artikel (Begleiter). Der bestimmte Artikel heißt "the". Er bedeutet „der", „die" oder „das".

1 Schreibe unter die Bilder das Nomen mit bestimmtem Artikel, so wie im Beispiel.

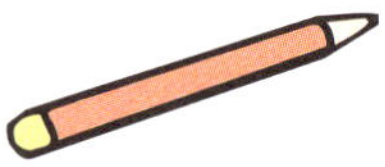
a) the pencil

b) ______

c) ______

d) ______

e) ______

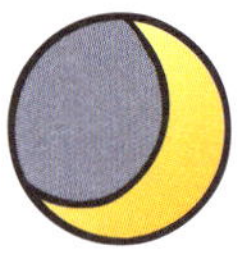
f) ______

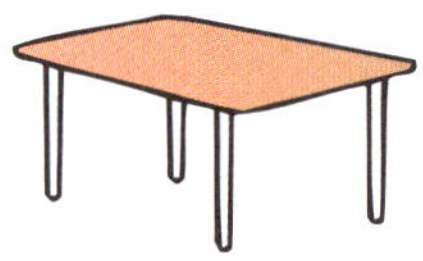
g) ______

h) ______

Der unbestimmte Artikel heißt im Englischen "a". Er bedeutet „ein" oder „eine".

a window a banana a farmer a teacher a doctor

2 Schreibe das richtige Nomen mit unbestimmtem Artikel unter die Bilder, so wie im Beispiel.

a) a dog

b) ______

c) ______

d) ______

e) ______

f) ______

g) ______

h) ______

Einige englische Nomen erscheinen ohne Artikel, zum Beispiel:

Mahlzeiten	Jahreszeiten
breakfast, lunch, dinner, supper	spring, summer, autumn, winter

"a" oder "an"?

Im Englischen werden einzelne Wörter beim Sprechen möglichst verbunden, besonders dann, wenn am Anfang des folgenden Wortes ein Vokal (Selbstlaut) gesprochen wird – a, e, i, o oder u. In solchen Fällen heißt der unbestimmte Artikel "an" und nicht "a".

an umbrella

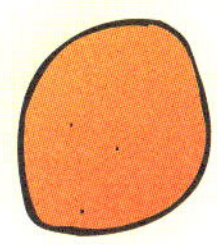
an orange

an apple

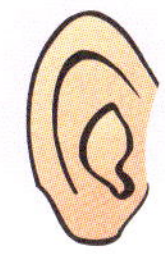
an ear

an elephant

an ice cream

an ape

an owl

1 Achte darauf, ob die Wörter mit einem Vokal beginnen oder nicht. Schreibe dann vor die Nomen den unbestimmten Artikel "a" oder "an".

a) ____ dog
b) ____ elephant
c) ____ cat
d) ____ ape

e) ____ sister
f) ____ uncle
g) ____ brother
h) ____ aunt

i) ____ orange
j) ____ banana
k) ____ tomato
l) ____ apple

2 Hier bestimmt das folgende Adjektiv, ob es "a" oder "an" heißt. Schreibe den richtigen unbestimmten Artikel auf, so wie im Beispiel.

a) a new house – an old house
b) ____ old man – ____ young man
c) ____ blue car – ____ orange car

Ob "a" oder "an" verwendet wird, richtet sich nach der Aussprache! Deshalb heißt es zum Beispiel "an hour" (eine Stunde) oder "a uniform" (eine Uniform). Bei allen Wörtern, die am Anfang mit einem Vokal ausgesprochen werden, ändert sich auch die Aussprache von "the". Lass es dir von jemandem erklären, der gut Englisch sprechen kann!

Der Plural mit -s

An ein Nomen, das im Singular (in der Einzahl) steht, muss man in der Regel ein -s anhängen, um den Plural (die Mehrzahl) zu bilden.

a cow

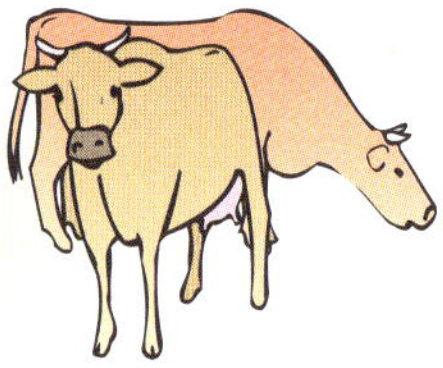
cows

a clock

clocks

an egg

eggs

1 Schreibe die Wörter, die hier im Singular stehen, im Plural auf und verbinde sie mit den richtigen Körperteilen.

a) ear ______________________
b) eye ______________________
c) lip ______________________
d) arm ______________________
e) hand ______________________
f) finger ______________________
g) shoulder ______________________
h) leg ______________________
i) knee ______________________

2 Unter jedem Bild steht der passende Begriff sowohl im Singular als auch im Plural. Streiche durch, was falsch ist.

a) girl / ~~girls~~

b) cup / cups

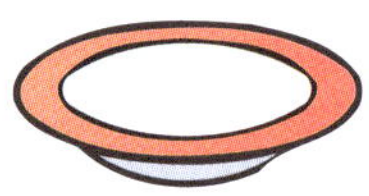
c) plate / plates

d) rabbit / rabbits

e) ring / rings

f) door / doors

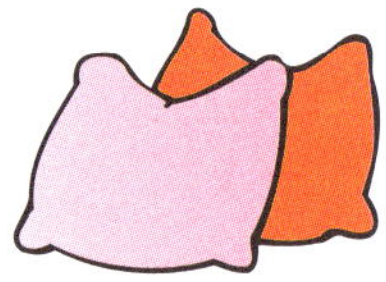
g) pillow / pillows

h) cloud / clouds

Der Plural mit -es

Es gibt einige englische Wörter, bei denen man zur Pluralbildung nicht nur -s, sondern -es anhängt. Man erkennt sie an ihren Endungen.

1 Wörter, die auf -s oder -x enden

a kiss

kisses

a fox

foxes

Bilde genauso den Plural dieser Wörter:

a) a box ______________ b) a bus ______________

c) a glass ______________ d) a dress ______________

2 Wörter, die auf -sh oder -ch enden

a bush

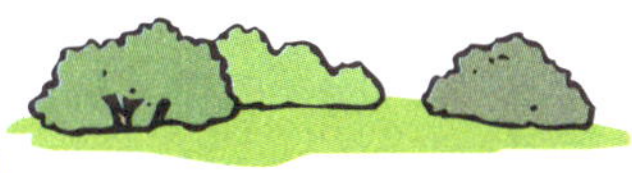
bushes

a coach

coaches

Bilde genauso den Plural dieser Wörter:

a) a watch ______________ b) a brush ______________

c) a dish ______________ d) a church ______________

3 Wörter, die auf -o enden. Bilde den Plural wie im Beispiel.

a) a hero heroes b) a potato ______________ c) a tomato ______________

Im Amerikanischen wird der Plural nach -o nur mit einfachem -s gebildet.

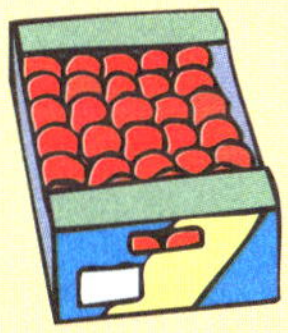
tomatoes (GB)

tomatos (USA)

potatoes (GB)

potatos (USA)

Besonderheiten bei der Pluralbildung

Bei einigen englischen Wörtern ändert sich der letzte Buchstabe, wenn man den Plural bildet.

1 Wörter, die auf -y enden
Bei den folgenden Wörtern ist im Singular der vorletzte Buchstabe ein Konsonant. Danach folgt ein -y. Im Plural enden solche Wörter dann auf -ies und das -y entfällt.

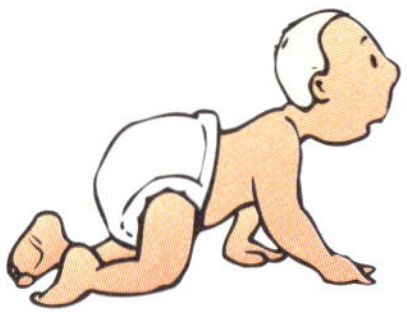
a baby

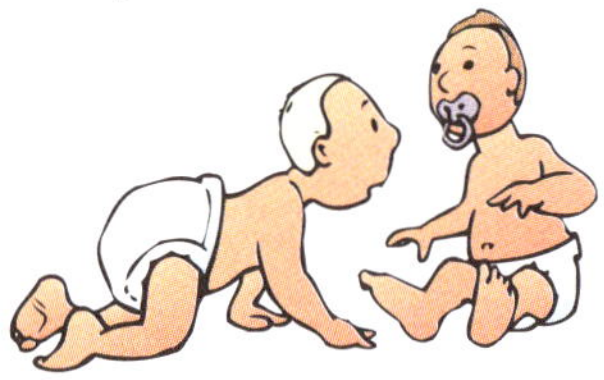
babies

a lady

ladies

Bilde genauso den Plural dieser Wörter:

a) a hobby ______________ b) a family ______________
c) a party ______________ d) a city ______________

Schon wieder eine Ausnahme: Wenn vor dem -y ein Vokal steht, dann wird ein -s angehängt, um den Plural zu bilden.

2 Mach es wie im Beispiel.

a) a toy toys b) a boy ______________ c) a key ______________

3 Wörter, die auf -f und -fe enden
Die folgenden Wörter enden im Singular auf -f oder -fe. Dann wird der Plural mit -ves gebildet, und das -f fällt weg.

a scarf...............scarves a knife..............knives

Bilde genauso den Plural dieser Wörter:

a) a life ______________ b) a thief ______________
c) a wife ______________ d) a shelf ______________

Ein paar Wörter sind im Singular und Plural gleich. Merke sie dir!
a hair.......hair a sheep......sheep a fish......fish

Unregelmäßige Pluralbildung

Manche Wörter haben einen besonderen Plural, den man sich einfach merken muss, zum Beispiel

man – men............woman – women............child – children

mouse – mice............foot – feet............tooth – teeth

1 Hier kannst du noch einmal Pluralformen üben, die auf den letzten vier Seiten besprochen wurden. Setze die Wörter in den Plural und sortiere sie.

city box cat day

family fish man bush baby fox

sheep watch mouse

boy

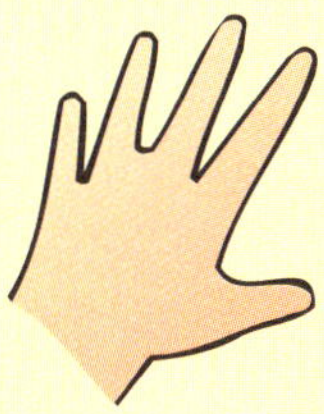

toy woman

key

finger foot

dog hair

tooth party hand child

Plural mit -s

Plural und Singular sind gleich

Unregelmäßiger Plural

Plural mit -ys nach -y und Vokal

Plural mit -es

Plural mit -ies nach -y und Konsonant

Der s-Genitiv im Singular

Wenn man ausdrücken will, dass jemandem etwas gehört, hängt man im Singular an den Namen der Person ein 's (ein s mit Apostroph) an.

Bob's cat

Susan's boyfriend

Mr Miller's daughter

1 Hier findest du jeweils den Namen einer Person und etwas, das zu dieser Person gehört. Drücke diese Zugehörigkeit mit dem s-Genitiv aus.

a) Mark – dog Mark's dog

b) Laura – sister ______________

c) Nick – car ______________

d) father – son ______________

e) Mary – horse ______________

f) Ben – guitar ______________

2 Hier siehst du jeweils ein Bild, neben dem mehrere Aussagen stehen. Lies sie genau durch. Nur eine passt genau zum Bild. Kreuze sie an.

a) Laura's dog is white and black.
b) Kevin's dog is white and black.
c) Kevin's cat is white and brown.
d) Laura's cat is white and brown.

a) Mrs Smith's daughter is nice.
b) Mrs Smith's son is nice.
c) Mrs Smith's daughter is ugly.
d) Mrs Smith's son is ugly.

a) Mr Brown's car is big and new.
b) Mr Brown's car is small and new.
c) Mr Brown's car is big and old.
d) Mr Brown's car is small und old.

Manchmal gehört etwas zwei Leuten gleichzeitig. Dann wird nur bei der zweiten Person das Genitiv-s angehängt!

Karin and Diana's horse   Henry and William's bike

Der s-Genitiv im Plural

Wenn ein Wort im Plural mit -s aufhört, dann wird beim Genitiv nur ein Apostroph (') angehängt.

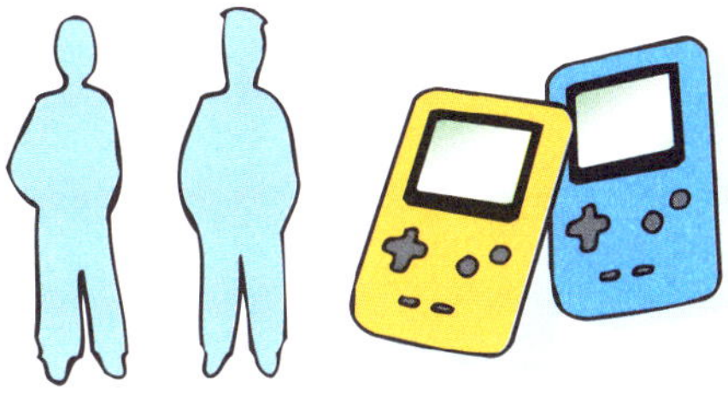

the friends' toys

the Millers' house

Wenn das Pluralwort aber mit einem anderen Buchstaben endet, wird beim Genitiv (genauso wie im Singular) das 's (s mit Apostroph) angehängt.

the children's school

the men's boats

1 Hier musst du entscheiden, ob der Genitiv mit 's oder nur mit ' (Apostroph) geschrieben wird.

a) the boys – books ______________________

b) the women – children ______________________

c) the girls – dolls ______________________

d) the teachers – pencils ______________________

e) the policemen – cars ______________________

f) the singers – song ______________________

g) the children – bikes ______________________

2 Lies die Sätze ganz genau durch. Kreuze den Satz an, der als einziger zum Bild passt.

a) The girls' bikes are pink and white.

b) The girl's bikes are pink and white.

c) The girls' bike is pink and white.

d) The girl's bike is pink and white.

Der Genitiv mit "of"

Wenn man ausdrücken will, dass etwas zu einer anderen Sache gehört, dann wird diese Zugehörigkeit im Englischen mit dem Wort "of" ausgedrückt.

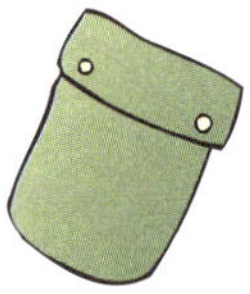
the pocket
+

the coat
=

the pocket of the coat

the wheels
+

the car
=

the wheels of the car

the clock
+

the church
=

the clock of the church

1 Verbinde die beiden Begriffe mit "of", um so ihre Zugehörigkeit auszudrücken.

a) the elephants – the zoo ______________________

b) the teachers – the school ______________________

c) the colours – the rainbow ______________________

d) the tower – the church ______________________

e) the name – the street ______________________

f) the brakes – the bike ______________________

2 Kreuze das Bild an, das zu dem Begriff passt.

?

the wheel of the bike

a)

b)

c)

d)

?

the head of an elephant

e)

f)

g)

h)

of-Genitiv und s-Genitiv

Der s-Genitiv wird verwendet, wenn einer Person etwas gehört. Der of-Genitiv drückt die Zugehörigkeit zu einer Sache aus. Den Unterschied zeigen dir diese Beispiele:

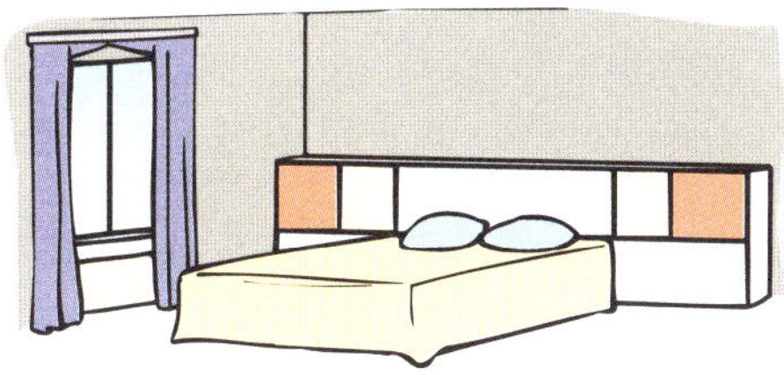

the parents' bedroom

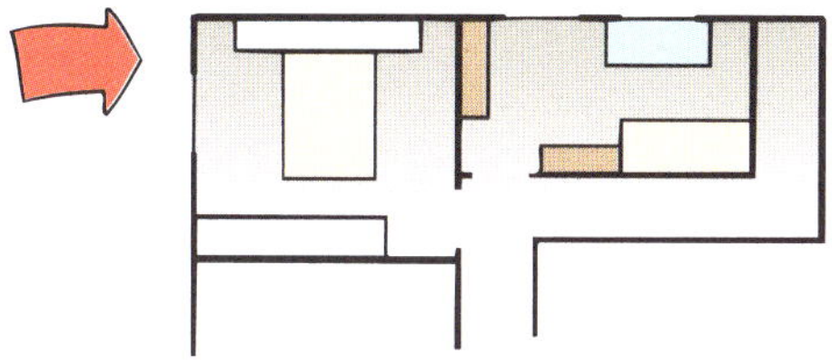

the bedroom of the house

Tom's book

the books of the library

1 Überlege dir bei den folgenden Beispielen, wann du den of-Genitiv verwenden musst und wann den s-Genitiv.

a) the mouse – the computer

____

b) the mouse – Jane

____

c) John – the monkey

____

d) the monkeys – the zoo

____

e) Mr Baker – the swimming pool

____

f) the swimming pool – the hotel

____

2 Unter jedem Bild stehen zwei Begriffe. Kreuze jeweils an, welcher richtig ist.

a) the name of the street
b) a child's name

c) Tim's shirt
d) the pocket of a shirt

Die Personalpronomen in der Subjektform

Wörter, die im Satz ein Nomen ersetzen können, nennt man Personalpronomen (persönliche Fürwörter).

I	ich
you	du
he, she, it	er, sie, es
we	wir
you	ihr
they	sie

Diese Personalpronomen ersetzen immer das Subjekt (den Satzgegenstand).

1 Setze in die Lücken die passenden Personalpronomen ein.

a) ____ am Kevin.

b) ____ are my friend.

c) ____ is my brother.
____ is my sister.
____ is his bike.

d) ____ are from Spain.

e) ____ are very nice!

f) ____ are very tired.

Im Englischen wird das Wort "you" einerseits für die Anrede von Kindern und Freunden verwendet, andererseits aber auch für die Anrede von unbekannten Erwachsenen.

Do you speak English?
Sprichst du Englisch?

Do you speak English?
Sprechen Sie Englisch?

"he", "she" oder "it"?

Im Englischen wird "he" und "she" nur bei Personen und Haustieren verwendet. Immer dann, wenn von Sachen gesprochen wird, muss man "it" verwenden, ebenso dann, wenn es sich um Tiere handelt, die keinen eigenen Namen haben.

1 Kreise unter jedem Bild ein, ob "he", "she" oder "it" gebraucht wird.

a) he she it

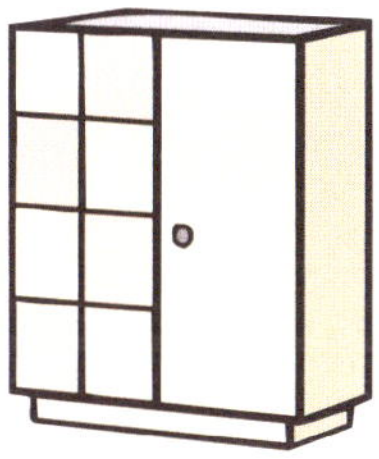

b) he she it

c) he she it

d) he she it

e) he she it

f) he she it

2 Hier werden auch die anderen Personalpronomen gesucht. Setze die passenden Wörter in die Lücken.

a) My name is Tanja. ____ am a girl. ____ am twelve.
b) Sally is nine. ____ is my sister. ____ is nice.
c) Harry is my brother. ____ is a little child. ____ is two.
d) My parents work every day. ____ are teachers.
e) Sally, Harry, my parents and I live together. ____ are a family.
f) My bike isn't new. ____ is very old.

Die Personalpronomen in der Objektform

Personalpronomen können auch als Akkusativ- oder als Dativ-Objekte verwendet werden. Im Englischen gibt es dabei im Unterschied zum Deutschen nur eine Objektform.

Personalpronomen als Dativ-Objekte

You give me the cake.	Du gibst mir den Kuchen.
I give you the cake.	Ich gebe dir den Kuchen.
I give him the cake.	Ich gebe ihm den Kuchen.
I give her the cake.	Ich gebe ihr den Kuchen.
I give it the cake (the cat).	Ich gebe ihr den Kuchen (der Katze).
I give us the cake.	Ich gebe uns den Kuchen.
I give you the cake.	Ich gebe euch den Kuchen.
I give them the cake.	Ich gebe ihnen den Kuchen.

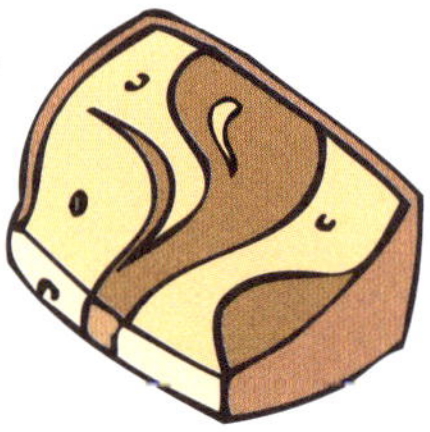

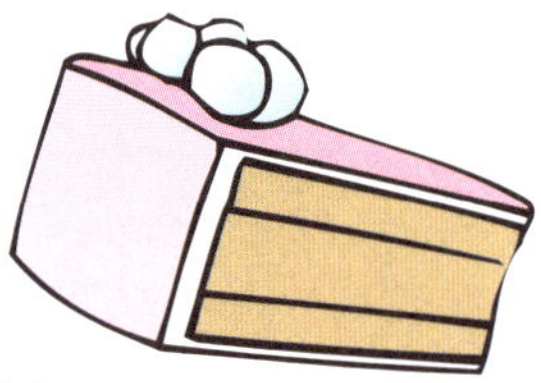

Personalpronomen als Akkusativ-Objekte

You can see me on the photo.	Du siehst mich auf dem Foto.
I can see you on the photo.	Ich sehe dich auf dem Foto.
I can see him on the photo.	Ich sehe ihn auf dem Foto.
I can see her on the photo.	Ich sehe sie auf dem Foto.
I can see it on the photo.	Ich sehe es auf dem Foto.
I can see us on the photo.	Ich sehe uns auf dem Foto.
I can see you on the photo.	Ich sehe euch auf dem Foto.
I can see them on the photo.	Ich sehe sie auf dem Foto.

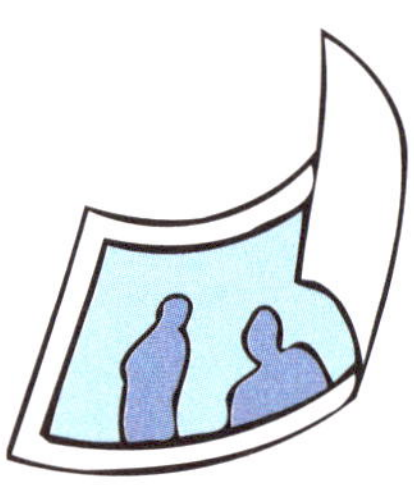

Weil die englischen Personalpronomen in der Objektform im Englischen nicht zwischen Dativ und Akkusativ unterscheiden, kannst du die Übersetzung dieser Wörter nur aus dem Satzzusammenhang erkennen.

1 Kreuze jeweils den einzigen Satz an, der genau zu dem Bild passt. Du musst dabei besonders auf die Personalpronomen achten.

a) The policeman can help her.
b) The policeman can help us.
c) The policeman can help him.
d) The policeman can help them.

a) The children can ask you.
b) The children can ask them.
c) The children can ask it.
d) The children can ask her.

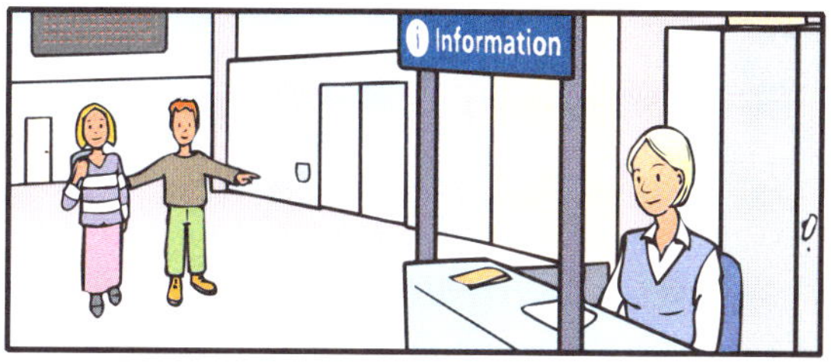

a) Give us the book, please.
b) Give me the book, please.
c) Give her the book, please.
d) Give them the book, please.

a) The car costs us a lot of money.
b) The car costs him a lot of money.
c) The car costs them a lot of money.
d) The car costs her a lot of money.

2 Setze die richtigen Personalpronomen ein.

it him them you me her

a) Jim is my friend. I often play with ________ .
b) This is Henry and Paul's book. Give it to ________ .
c) My friend asks ________ what time it is.
d) You are nice. I like ________ .
e) The tea is for your mother. I will take ________ to ________ .

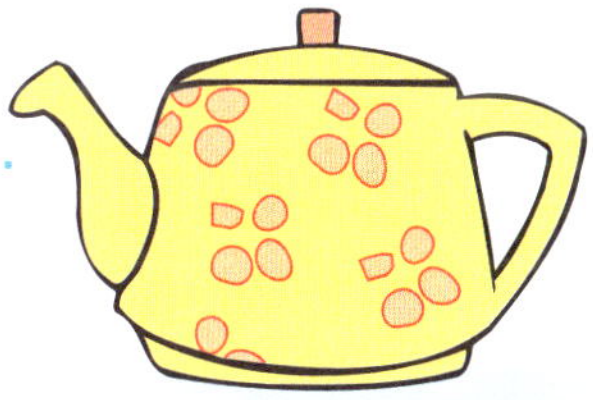

Die Possessivbegleiter

Wörter, die den Besitz oder eine Zugehörigkeit ausdrücken, nennt man Possessivbegleiter (besitzanzeigende Begleiter). Sie stehen immer vor einem Nomen.

My chair is red.
Your chair is green.
His chair is blue.
Her chair is yellow.
Its chair is white.

Our car is brown.
Your car is pink.
Their car is black.

1 Schreibe in die Lücken die richtigen Possessivbegleiter.

a) This is ______ hamster.

b) This is ______ new teacher.

c) This is ______ house.

d) Can I have ______ book, please?

e) The cat is in ______ basket.

f) My friend and ______ sister.

2 Streiche in jedem Satz den Possessivbegleiter durch, der nicht passt.

a) Jane and Jill are sisters. Their/Our last name is Johnson.
b) This is my hamster. It is in his/its cage.
c) She is my friend. His/Her name is Sarah.
d) My friends and I like to play football. Mr Smith is our/their coach.

Die Possessivpronomen

Possessivpronomen (besitzanzeigende Fürwörter) drücken ebenfalls aus, dass jemand etwas besitzt oder dass es ihm gehört. Possessivpronomen stehen aber ohne Nomen.

	my			mine.
	your			yours.
	his			his.
It is	her	house.	It is	hers.
	our			ours.
	your			yours.
	their			theirs.

1 Kreuze jeweils den Satz an, der genau zum Bild passt.

a) My bag is brown. Yours is pink.
b) Your bag is brown. Hers is green.
c) Your bag is brown. Mine is black.
d) My bag is black. His is blue.

a) His car is small. Ours is big.
b) Her car is big. Mine is small.
c) Her car is big. Ours is small.
d) Our car is big. Hers is small.

a) His bike is old. Ours is new.
b) My bike is old. Yours is new.
c) Their bike is old. Yours is new.
d) His bike is old. Hers is new.

2 Setze in die folgenden Sätze die richtigen Possessivbegleiter oder Possessivpronomen ein.

ours — its — our — my — mine — his

a) I like ______ bike.
b) We like to learn English. Miss Snuggs is ______ teacher.
c) This is Kevin. ______ football is black and white.
d) Look, there is a cat in ______ basket!
e) Your pen is yellow. ______ is pink.
f) Your house is big. ______ is small.

Häufige Verben

Verben sagen uns, was jemand macht oder tut. Man nennt sie deshalb auch Tätigkeitswörter. Im Englischen steht vor Verben im Infinitiv (in der Grundform) immer ein "to"; „machen" heißt zum Beispiel "to make", „spielen" heißt "to play". Hier findest du einige Verben, die ganz häufig gebraucht werden. Du solltest sie alle gut kennen.

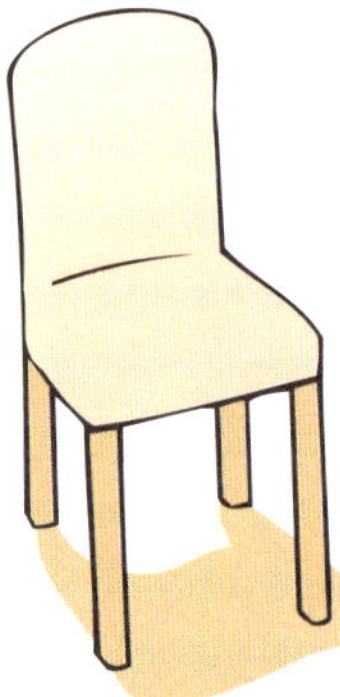

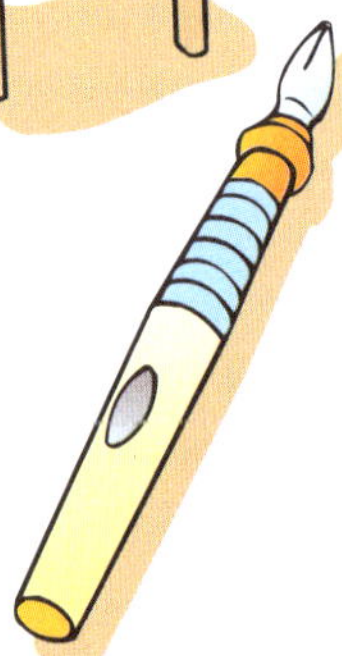

to sit (sitzen)
to go (gehen)
to run (rennen)
to drive (fahren)
to swim (schwimmen)
to come (kommen)

to work (arbeiten)
to play (spielen)
to read (lesen)
to write (schreiben)
to draw (zeichnen)
to sleep (schlafen)
to dream (träumen)

to say (sagen)
to speak (sprechen)
to shout (rufen)
to ask (fragen)
to answer (antworten)
to sing (singen)

to eat (essen)
to drink (trinken)
to cook (kochen)

1 Schreibe unter jedes Bild das Verb, das am besten dazu passt.

a) ____________

b) ____________

c) ____________

d) ____________

e) ____________

f) ____________

g) ____________

h) ____________

2 Welches Verb passt nicht zu den anderen? Streiche es durch.

a) to go – to run – to eat – to drive

b) to speak – to shout – to ask – to sleep – to answer

c) to draw – to write – to drink – to read

Das Verb "to do"

Das englische Verb "to do" bedeutet im Deutschen „tun, machen". Dies sind die Formen mit den dazugehörigen Personalpronomen:

I do you do he does she does it does we do you do they do

Es gibt einige feste Verbindungen von "to do" mit Nomen, deren Bedeutung man sich merken muss:

She does her homework.	Sie macht ihre Hausaufgaben.
He does the cooking.	Er kocht das Essen.
We do our jobs.	Wir erledigen unsere Arbeiten.
She does the shopping.	Sie kauft ein.

Bei der Verneinung wird "not" hinter das Verb "to do" gesetzt. Dabei gibt es eine Langform und eine Kurzform. Die Langform findet man vor allem in der Schriftsprache. In der gesprochenen Sprache wird die Kurzform verwendet, aber mittlerweile auch in vielen Texten.

Langform		**Kurzform**	
I do not		I don't	
you do not		you don't	
he does not		he doesn't	
she does not	play	she doesn't	play
it does not		it doesn't	
we do not		we don't	
you do not		you don't	
they do not		they don't	

In vielen Fällen werden im Englischen Aussagesätze verneint, indem man vor das Verb "don't" oder "doesn't" setzt, so wie hier:

I don't like coffee. He doesn't like tea.

1 Setze richtig "don't" oder "doesn't" ein.

a) He ________ like apples. b) I ________ like milk.

c) The cat ________ like its food. d) We ________ like monsters.

2 Welcher Satz passt zum Bild?

a) She does the shopping.

b) She does her homework.

c) She does the cooking.

d) She does her job.

Das Verb "can"

Das englische Verb "can" hat keinen Infinitiv. Es hat im Deutschen die Bedeutung „können" oder „dürfen". Sämtliche Formen des Verbs sind im Präsens gleich.

I can.....you can......he can.....she can.....it can.....
we can.....you can.....they can

Bei der verneinten Form wird unmittelbar an das "can" ein "not" angehängt – "cannot".
Die Kurzform der Verneinung heißt "can't".

Auch bei der Verneinung sind alle Formen gleich:

I, you, he, she, it, we, you, they – cannot. Und in der Kurzform: can't.

1 Die Flaggen weisen dich auf sechs verschiedene Sprachen hin. Schreibe auf, welche Sprache jede Person sprechen kann. Schreibe auch eine Sprache auf, die sie nicht sprechen kann. Bitte aufpassen – Sprachen werden genau wie Ländernamen großgeschrieben!

English French Spanish Turkish Russian Italian

a) Bill can speak English. He can't speak ______________________
b) Carmen ______________________
c) Achmed ______________________
d) Irina ______________________
e) Pierre ______________________
f) Mario ______________________

Wenn etwas ganz ausdrücklich verboten ist, heißt es "must not" oder in der Kurzform "mustn't".

Das Verb "to be"

Das Verb "to be" entspricht dem deutschen Verb „sein". In Verbindung mit den Personalpronomen gibt es eine Langform und eine Kurzform. Die Langform wird vor allem in der Schriftsprache verwendet. Die Kurzform wird vor allem beim Sprechen verwendet, man findet sie aber auch zunehmend in geschriebenen Texten. Hier findest du alle Formen von "to be" im Präsens (in der Gegenwartsform).

Langform		Kurzform	
I am		I'm	
you are		you're	
he is		he's	
she is	eleven	she's	eleven
it is		it's	
we are		we're	
you are		you're	
they are		they're	

In der verneinten Form wird "not" ergänzt. "I am not old" heißt also „ich bin nicht alt". Auch hier gibt es eine Langform und eine Kurzform.

Langform		Kurzform	
I am not		I'm not	
you are not		you aren't	
he is not		he isn't	
she is not	old	she isn't	old
it is not		it isn't	
we are not		we aren't	
you are not		you aren't	
they are not		they aren't	

1 Schreibe die folgenden Sätze noch einmal und verwende dabei die Kurzform oder die verneinte Kurzform von "to be".

a) I / to be / a boy — I'm a boy. ____________________
b) You / to be / a nice girl. ____________________
c) It / to be / not / a dog. ____________________
d) I / to be / not / thirteen. ____________________
e) He / to be / a tall man. ____________________
f) We / to be / not / very hungry. ____________________

Das Verb "to have"

Dem deutschen Verb „haben, besitzen“ entspricht im Englischen das Verb “to have”. Im Präsens heißt es aber immer “have got”. Wie bei “to do” und “to be” gibt es auch bei “to have” eine Langform, hauptsächlich in der Schriftsprache, und eine Kurzform, die grundsätzlich beim Sprechen und immer häufiger in geschriebenen Texten verwendet wird.

Langform		**Kurzform**	
I have got		I’ve got	
you have got		you’ve got	
he has got		he’s got	
she has got	a ball	she’s got	a ball
it has got		it’s got	
we have got		we’ve got	
you have got		you’ve got	
they have got		they’ve got	

In der verneinten Form wird “not” zwischen “have” und “got” eingeschoben.

Langform		**Kurzform**	
I have not got		I haven’t got	
you have not got		you haven’t got	
he has not got		he hasn’t got	
she has not got	a tiger	she hasn’t got	a tiger
it has not got		it hasn’t got	
we have not got		we haven’t got	
you have not got		you haven’t got	
they have not got		they haven’t got	

1 Was haben die Leute, was haben sie nicht? Schau dir die Bilder an und schreibe die richtigen Sätze auf, so wie im Beispiel. In der Klammer am Anfang des Satzes steht das Personalpronomen, das du verwenden sollst.

a) (You) You’ve got a ball. You haven’t got a tiger.

b) (We) ______________________________

c) (They) ______________________________

d) (I) ______________________________

e) (She) ______________________________

"to have" bildet oft mit Nomen eine feste Einheit, deren Bedeutung man nicht wörtlich übersetzen kann. Man muss sich die Bedeutung merken. Hier sind einige Beispiele:

to have breakfast – frühstücken
to have lunch – zu Mittag essen
to have dinner – Abendbrot essen
to have a shower – duschen
to have a bath – baden
to have a drink – etwas trinken
to have a cup of tea – eine Tasse Tee trinken
to have a party – feiern
to have fun – Spaß haben

Außerdem drückt man im Englischen mit "to have" aus, dass etwas getan werden muss. Dann folgt ein Infinitiv mit "to", so wie in diesen Beispielen:

I have to wash my car.

You have to take your medicine.

1 Schreibe unter die folgenden Bilder, was dort getan wird. Achte auf die richtige Form von "to have" in der 3. Person Singular.

a) He ______________________

b) We ______________________

c) They ______________________

d) She ______________________

2 Peter muss eine Menge Dinge erledigen. Schreibe Sätze wie im ersten Beispiel.

a) He has to do his homework.
b) He ______________________ (check his computer)
c) He ______________________ (visit his grandmother)
d) He ______________________ (tidy up his room)
e) He ______________________ (go to the doctor)
f) He ______________________ (call his friend)

Die Verlaufsform der Gegenwart - present progressive

Wenn man Handlungen beschreiben will, die gerade stattfinden und die noch nicht beendet sind, verwendet man im Englischen die Verlaufsform der Gegenwart (present progressive). Sie wird so gebildet:

Nomen oder Personalpronomen	Form von "to be"	Verb in der -ing-Form
The cat	is	sleeping.
You	are	jumping.
We	are	playing.
The bird	is	singing.
I	am	calling.
He	is	working.

1 Schreibe Sätze in der Verlaufsform. Verwende die angegebenen Personalpronomen und Verben. Du kannst entweder die Kurzform (I'm) oder die Langform (I am) verwenden.

a) (I – repair my bike) ______________________________
b) (You – watch TV) ______________________________
c) (He – talk) ______________________________
d) (They – play football) ______________________________
e) (You – sing together) ______________________________
f) (We – read a book) ______________________________

2 Welcher Satz passt zu dem jeweiligen Bild? Kreuze ihn an.

a) He's eating a banana.
b) She's reading a book.
c) It's eating a banana.
d) We're eating a banana.

a) We're reading comics.
b) We're playing football.
c) We're playing tennis.
d) He's reading comics.

a) He's repairing his bike.
b) He's washing his car.
c) She's repairing her bike.
d) She's washing her car.

Besondere -ing-Formen

Manche Verben verändern sich etwas, wenn man die -ing-Form bildet.

Bei Verben mit einem -e am Ende, das man nicht mitspricht, verschwindet das -e bei der -ing-Form, zum Beispiel bei:

to make – making
to write – writing
to come – coming
to give – giving
to live – living
to dance – dancing
to ride – riding
to drive – driving

Wenn ein kurz gesprochener und betonter Selbstlaut (a, e, i, o, u) vor einem einfachen Mitlaut am Ende des Infinitivs steht, wird dieser Mitlaut bei der -ing-Form verdoppelt, zum Beispiel bei:

to run – running
to put – putting
to sit – sitting
to swim – swimming
to stop – stopping
to shop – shopping
to begin – beginning

Aus einem -ie am Ende des Worts wird bei der -ing-Form ein -y, zum Beispiel:

to die – dying
to lie – lying

1 Schreibe hinter jedes Verb in der -ing-Form die Grundform. Beachte dabei die Ausnahmeregeln.

a) writing to write ____________
b) swimming ____________
c) riding ____________
d) stopping ____________
e) beginning ____________
f) making ____________

2 Bilde von den folgenden Verben die -ing-Form. Beachte dabei die Ausnahmeregeln.

a) (to sit) ____________
b) (to shop) ____________
c) (to give) ____________
d) (to come) ____________
e) (to lie) ____________
f) (to live) ____________

Im Deutschen gibt es keine Verlaufsform. Beim Übersetzen ergänzt man am besten das Wort „gerade“.

I'm playing. Ich spiele gerade.

Die Verneinung in der Verlaufsform

Die Verneinung wird in der Verlaufsform gebildet, indem die Form des Verbs "to be" durch das Anhängen von "not" verneint wird (vgl. dazu die entsprechende Langform und Kurzform auf Seite 31).

He is not working, he's swimming.

We aren't eating, we are sleeping.

1 Schreibe Sätze in der verneinten Verlaufsform. Verwende die angegebenen Namen bzw. Personalpronomen und die Verben. Du kannst entweder die Kurzform (you aren't) oder die Langform (you are not) verwenden.

a) (I – work) I'm not working.
b) (We – play cards) ______
c) (You – dance) ______
d) (Mrs Bucks – come) ______
e) (The women – shop) ______
f) (She – sing) ______
g) (The bird – fly) ______
h) (Pete – ride his bike) ______

2 Welcher Satz passt zum Bild? Kreuze ihn an.

a) The sun is shining. It isn't raining.
b) It is raining, and the sun is shining.
c) It isn't raining, and the sun isn't shining.
d) The sun isn't shining. It is raining.

a) She isn't doing the cooking. She's watching TV.
b) She isn't doing the cooking. She's swimming.
c) She isn't watching TV. She's doing the cooking.
d) She isn't watching TV. She's swimming.

Der Imperativ

Der Imperativ (die Befehlsform) wird benutzt, um eine Anweisung zu geben oder um etwas zu verbieten. Der Imperativ hat im Englischen dieselbe Form wie der Infinitiv ohne "to".

Sit down!

Come back!

Wenn es sich nicht um direkte Befehle handelt, setzt man vor oder hinter den Imperativ fast immer das höfliche "please". Im Gegensatz zum Deutschen wird beim Imperativ im Englischen meist kein Ausrufezeichen gesetzt, sondern ein Punkt.

Be quiet, please.

Shut the door, please.

Wenn jemand etwas nicht tun soll, setzt man vor den Imperativ "do not" bzw. in der Kurzform "don't".

Don't cry, please.

Please, don't go.

Mit dem Imperativ "let us" bzw. der Kurzform "let's" wird aufgefordert, etwas gemeinsam zu tun.

Let's dance.

Let's go for a walk.

1 Nur ein Satz passt jeweils zum Bild. Kreuze ihn an.

a) Don't smoke, please.

b) Don't drink, please.

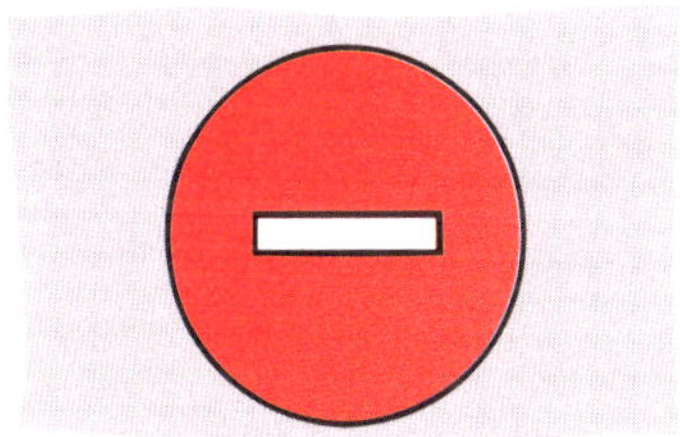

c) Don't enter!

d) Come back!

Die einfache Gegenwart - simple present

Neben der Verlaufsform der Gegenwart gibt es im Englischen auch die einfache Gegenwart (simple present). Sie entspricht in allen Formen dem Infinitiv, außer in der 3. Person Singular, also bei einzelnen Dingen und Personen und bei “he”, “she” und “it”. Dann wird an die Grundform noch ein -s angehängt, wie hier in diesen Beispielen.

I live	I sleep
you live	you sleep
he lives	John sleeps
she lives	Diana sleeps
it lives	the cat sleeps
we live	we sleep
you live	you sleep
they live	they sleep

Die einfache Gegenwart wird im Englischen immer dann verwendet, wenn eine Handlung immer wieder regelmäßig stattfindet – oder nie. Deshalb gibt es einige Wörter, die darauf hinweisen, dass man die einfache Gegenwart verwenden muss, zum Beispiel:

always (immer)	often (oft, häufig)	sometimes (manchmal)
usually (üblicherweise)	seldom, rarely (selten)	never (niemals)

1 Entscheide, ob hier jeweils in der einfachen Gegenwart ein -s angehängt wird oder nicht.

a) Linda (eat) ____________ b) The baby (sleep) ____________
c) We (swim) ____________ d) She (drive) ____________
e) You (work) ____________ f) My friends (dance) ____________
g) I (read) ____________ h) He (paint) ____________

2 Setze in die folgenden Sätze das Verb in der einfachen Gegenwart ein. Achte darauf, ob du ein -s anhängen musst. Gebrauche die angegebenen Verben.

drink go play smoke go

a) We usually ________ on holiday in June.
b) My uncle sometimes ________ his pipe.
c) I always ________ to bed at ten.
d) The English usually ________ tea.
e) The Bakers often ________ tennis in the afternoon.

Die einfache Gegenwart wird auch bei Gefühlsäußerungen verwendet, zum Beispiel:

She loves you.

I hate this music.

Zudem wird die einfache Gegenwart zur Beschreibung immerwährender Tatsachen eingesetzt:

In England it often rains in winter.

The sun rises every morning.

Schließlich verwendet man die einfache Gegenwart dann, wenn man mehrere aufeinanderfolgende Handlungen beschreibt. Darauf weisen oft die folgenden Wörter hin:

first (zuerst) then (dann) after that (danach) finally (schließlich)

1 Hier soll beschrieben werden, wie Sarah zur Schule kommt. Die Begriffe sind aber durcheinandergeraten. Ordne sie in die richtige Reihenfolge und schreibe sie dann auf. Denke daran, das -s bei den Verben zu ergänzen.

ride to school | say goodbye to her mum | take her bike | enter the classroom

a) First Sarah ______________________
b) Then she ______________________
c) After that she ______________________
d) Finally she ______________________

2 Hier wird beschrieben, was Ken morgens tut. Bringe die Begriffe in die richtige Reihenfolge und schreibe sie auf. Denke ans -s beim Verb.

brush his teeth | have breakfast | awake | put on his clothes

a) First Ken ______________________
b) Then he ______________________
c) After that he ______________________
d) Finally he ______________________

Die Verneinung in der einfachen Gegenwart

Im Englischen können nur Hilfsverben wie "to be", "to have" oder "can" durch das Anhängen von "not" verneint werden. Zur Verneinung aller anderen Verben in der einfachen Gegenwart gebraucht man "do not (don't)" bzw. "does not (doesn't)".

I don't play football.
You don't like coffee.
He doesn't drive a car.
She doesn't drink beer.
It doesn't sleep in its basket.

We don't write books.
You don't read newspapers.
They don't swim in their swimming pool.

1 Schreibe jeweils einen verneinten Satz, so wie im Beispiel.

a) Jenny plays football. Bill doesn't play football.
b) I go to school. You ______________________
c) I like tea. Mrs Smith ______________________
d) We work in the garden. You ______________________
e) Our cat likes milk. Our dog ______________________
f) The children swim. Their parents ______________________
g) My father smokes. My mother ______________________

2 Kreuze den Satz an, der jeweils zum Bild passt.

a) Eva likes ice cream and she likes fish and chips.
b) Eva doesn't like ice cream. She likes fish and chips.
c) Eva likes ice cream. She doesn't like fish and chips.
d) Eva doesn't like fish and chips and she doesn't like ice cream.

a) Tom plays the guitar. He plays the piano, too.
b) Tom plays the piano. He doesn't play the guitar.
c) Tom plays the guitar. He doesn't play the piano.
d) Tom doesn't play the guitar. He doesn't play the piano, either.

Wenn "to do" oder "to have" in festen Verbindungen auftauchen, werden sie ebenso mit "don't" bzw. "doesn't" verneint.

He doesn't have breakfast.
We don't do the shopping.
She doesn't have a bath.

Verlaufsform und einfache Gegenwart im Vergleich

Beim Unterscheiden von Verlaufsform und einfacher Gegenwart helfen folgende Fragen:

Verlaufsform
Passiert etwas eben gerade jetzt?

Linda is writing a letter.
She isn't eating.

I'm drinking milk.
I'm not drinking beer.

Einfache Gegenwart
Passiert etwas immer, selten oder nie?

Linda often writes letters.
She doesn't write books.

I often drink coffee with sugar.
But I don't drink coffee with milk.

1 Entscheide, ob du die Verlaufsform oder die einfache Gegenwart verwenden musst.

a) Every morning Pete ______________ (get up) at 8 o'clock.
b) Kate ______________ (wait) for the bus at the moment.
c) Mr Brown ______________ (read) the newspaper now.
d) Diana always ______________ (meet) her friends at the bus stop.
e) Robin never ______________ (sleep) before ten o'clock.
f) The birds ______________ (sing) now.
g) I cannot go into the bathroom now because my sister ______________ (brush) her teeth.

2 Schreibe einen zweiten Satz, der verneint ist. Achte darauf, ob die Verlaufsform oder die einfache Gegenwart verwendet wird.

a) I often eat bread and butter. I ______________ fish and chips.
b) You're drinking orange juice. You ______________ water.
c) George always sleeps at night. He ______________ at school.
d) Mrs Smith drives a car. She ______________ a bus.
e) Ken is doing his homework. He ______________ the shopping.

Präpositionen des Ortes

Um zu beschreiben, in welchem Verhältnis sich eine Sache zu einer anderen befindet, gebraucht man Präpositionen (Verhältniswörter). Am deutlichsten wird das bei den Präpositionen des Ortes.

1 Schau dir die Zeichnung an. Setze dann in die folgenden Sätze die richtigen Präpositionen ein: in front of, over, on, under, behind.

a) Our dog is lying ______________________ the chair.
b) The car is ____________________ the house.
c) My sister is ____________________ the tree.
d) I'm sitting _______________________ the roof.
e) A bird is flying ________________________ me.

2 Welcher Satz ist richtig? Kreuze ihn an.

a) Bill is over the bike.
b) Bill is behind the bike.
c) Bill is on the bike.
d) Bill is under the bike.

a) The parrot is near the cage.
b) The parrot is behind the cage.
c) The parrot is in front of the cage.
d) The parrot is on the cage.

a) The sheep is behind the box.
b) The sheep is under the box.
c) The sheep is on the box.
d) The sheep is in the box.

Redewendungen mit "in" und "on"

Präpositionen können oft nicht unmittelbar ins Deutsche übersetzt werden. Ihre Bedeutung hängt von der Redewendung ab, in der sie gebraucht werden. Man merkt sie sich am besten als feststehenden Begriff.

in

in the picture – auf dem Bild
in the sky – am Himmel
in the street – auf der Straße
in the world – auf der Welt
in bed – im Bett
in German – auf Deutsch

on

on the floor – auf dem Boden
on the coast – an der Küste
on my way – unterwegs
on the train – im Zug
on TV – im Fernsehen
on the radio – im Radio
on the phone – am Telefon
to go on foot – zu Fuß gehen
on the left – links
on the right – rechts

A

B
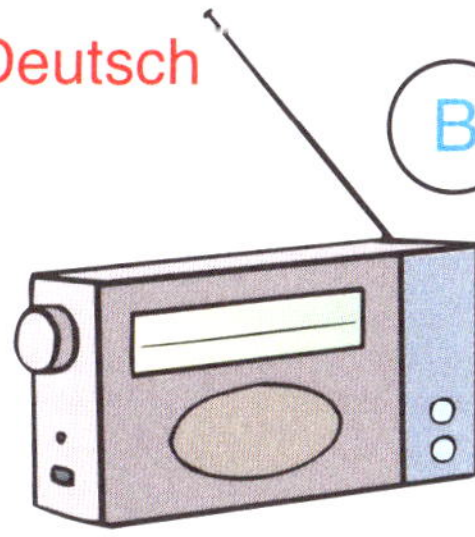

D

C

E

F

G

H

I

L

J

K

1 Schreibe zum jeweiligen Buchstaben die entsprechende Redewendung auf.

a) ______________________ b) ______________________
c) ______________________ d) ______________________
e) ______________________ f) ______________________
g) ______________________ h) ______________________
i) ______________________ j) ______________________
k) ______________________ l) ______________________

Präpositionen der Richtung

Mit den Präpositionen der Richtung wird ausgedrückt, wohin sich jemand bewegt.

1 Schau dir das Bild oben genau an. Kreuze die Sätze an, die nicht zum Bild passen.

a) The cat is climbing up the tree.
b) The bird is sitting on the wall.
c) The dog is barking under the tree.
d) Bill is coming from the house.
e) Sarah is going round the car.
f) Bob is going to the house.
g) The lorry is driving over the bridge.
h) The bike is standing under the tree.
i) Mary is walking across the street.
j) The car is driving over the bridge.

2 Unterscheide “in” und “into” (hinein) und setze sie richtig ein.

a) We are going __________ the house.
b) Fish swim __________ the river.
c) Let’s go __________ the cathedral.
d) You have to turn left __________ Cleve Road.
e) Look, there are three mice __________ your old car.
f) I like milk __________ my coffee.

Die Präposition “to” taucht oft in Redewendungen auf und muss jeweils unterschiedlich übersetzt werden.

to go to bed – ins Bett gehen
to go to school – zur Schule gehen
to go to Scotland – nach Schottland fahren
to write a letter to somebody – jemandem einen Brief schreiben
Welcome to London! – Willkommen in London!
an answer to a question – eine Antwort auf eine Frage

Präpositionen der Zeit

Wie viele andere lassen sich auch die Präpositionen der Zeit nicht wörtlich übersetzen, sodass man sie sich am besten im Zusammenhang mit den feststehenden Begriffen merkt.

John usually goes to bed **before** eleven.
It's fifteen minutes **to** seven.

Let's meet **after** lunch.
It's a quarter **past** ten.

in the beginning – am Anfang
in winter – im Winter
in April – im April

on Sunday – am Sonntag
on 18th June – am 18. Juni
on your birthday – an deinem Geburtstag

at 5 o'clock – um fünf Uhr
at the end – am Schluss
at Christmas – zu Weihnachten
at the moment – im Moment

at the weekend – am Wochenende
at night – nachts
at Easter – zu Ostern
at the same time – zur gleichen Zeit

1 Setze die richtigen Präpositionen ein.

a) My birthday is ________ 2nd October.
b) It's half ________ seven.
c) School starts ________ 8 o'clock.
d) ________ Thursdays I usually play football.
e) Children have to sleep ________ night.

2 Welcher feststehende Begriff mit Präposition passt zu dem jeweiligen Bild?

a) ________________

b) ________________

c) ________________

d) ________________

e) ________________

f) ________________

Bei allgemeinen Tageszeiten steht die Präposition "in".
Ist die Tageszeit näher bestimmt, verwendet man "on".

in the morning – vormittags, morgens
in the afternoon – nachmittags
in the evening – abends

on Friday morning
on Wednesday afternoon
on Christmas eve

Häufige Adjektive

Adjektive (Eigenschaftswörter) beschreiben genauer, wie eine Sache oder eine Person ist. Hier findest du einige Adjektive, die ganz häufig gebraucht werden. Du solltest sie gut kennen.

red.....blue.....green.....yellow.....orange.....white.....black.....grey.....pink.....brown

quick – schnell
slow – langsam
loud – laut
quiet – ruhig
young – jung
old – alt
new – neu

big – groß
small – klein
nice – nett
ugly – hässlich
happy – glücklich
sad – traurig
high – hoch

1 Schreibe unter jede Tube das Farb-Adjektiv.

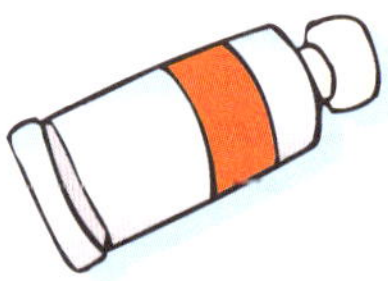
a) ____________________

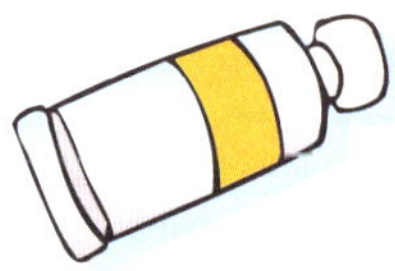
b) ____________________

c) ____________________

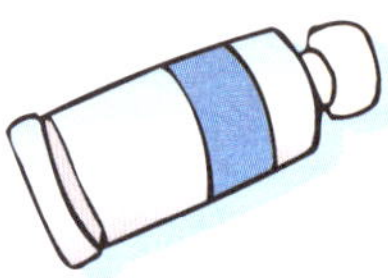
d) ____________________

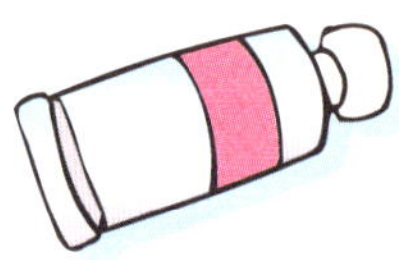
e) ____________________

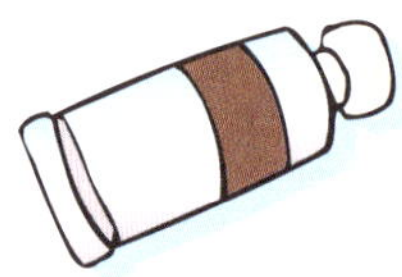
f) ____________________

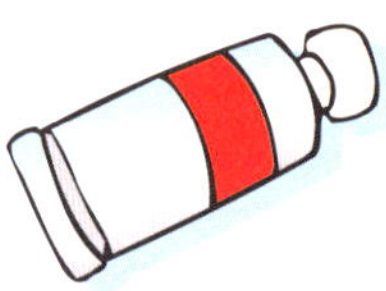
g) ____________________

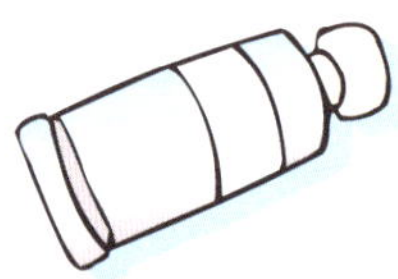
h) ____________________

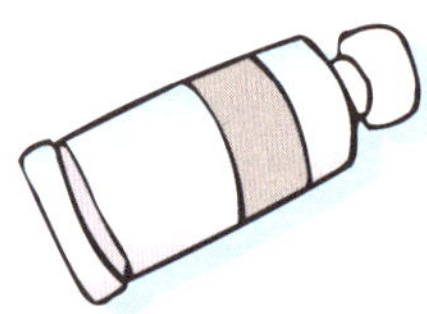
i) ____________________

2 Neben jedem Bild stehen zwei Adjektive. Streiche das Wort durch, das nicht zu dem Bild passt.

a) ugly / nice

b) small / big

c) young / old

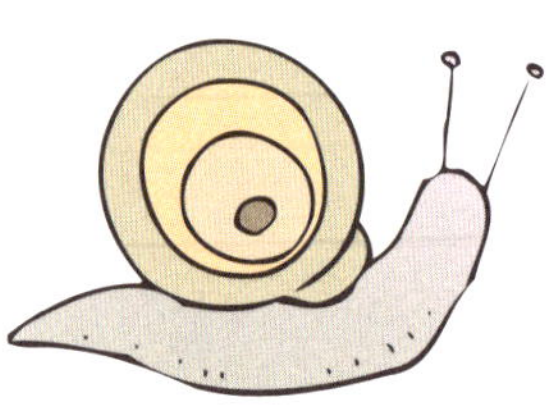
d) quick / slow

e) loud / quiet

f) happy / sad

Adjektive und Nomen

Adjektive stehen direkt vor dem Nomen. Dabei können mehrere Adjektive nacheinander folgen. Anders als im Deutschen haben die Adjektive im Englischen immer die gleiche Form.

We've got an old red car.	... ein altes rotes Auto.
Mrs Black is a nice old lady.	... eine nette alte Dame.
Mr Kelly is a sad old man.	... ein trauriger alter Mann.

Wenn Adjektive direkt beim Nomen stehen, nennt man das die attributive Verwendung des Adjektivs. Adjektive können aber auch nach einer Form von "to be" stehen, um die Eigenschaft einer Person oder einer Sache zu beschreiben. Das nennt man die prädikative Verwendung des Adjektivs.

Attributiv	**Prädikativ**
She is a nice girl.	The girl is nice.
I'm listening to a great song.	This song is great!
I've got an awful sister.	My sister is awful.

1 Neben jedem Bild stehen drei Adjektive. Nur zwei davon passen. Schreibe diese beiden Adjektive und das Nomen so wie im Beispiel auf.

a) a little brown mouse

b) ______

c) ______

d) ______

2 Bilde einen Satz, in dem das Adjektiv prädikativ gebraucht wird, so wie im Beispiel.

a) the red ball — The ball is red.

b) the tall boy ______

c) the loud music ______

d) the brown horse ______

e) the red tomato ______

Alle Adjektive, die sich auf Ländernamen beziehen, werden großgeschrieben.

an English boy — an Italian pizza — Danish ice cream

Adverbien der Häufigkeit

Ein Wort, das etwas Näheres über ein Verb aussagt, nennt man Adverb. Die Adverbien der Häufigkeit geben genauer an, wie oft etwas geschieht.

usually – normalerweise
often – oft
always – immer
already – schon
just – gerade
seldom, rarely – selten
never – niemals
sometimes – manchmal
hardly – kaum
soon – bald

Wenn das Verb eine Form von "to be" ist, dann steht das Adverb der Häufigkeit immer nach dem Verb.

He is never sad. I'm just playing. The children are always happy.

Sonst steht das Adverb der Häufigkeit immer vor dem Verb.

I never drink coffee.
They sometimes go into the garden.
Jim always does the shopping.
I usually get up early.

Bei Sätzen mit dem Hilfsverb "can" steht das Adverb zwischen "can" und dem Vollverb.

The little boy can hardly walk. My brother can already drive a car.

1 Hier sind Satzteile durcheinandergeraten. Schreibe sie in der richtigen Reihenfolge auf, so wie im Beispiel.

a) her parents / often / Patty / helps
Patty often helps her parents.

b) sometimes / Bob / play / tennis
____

c) just / I'm / reading / a book
____

2 Welches Adverb der Häufigkeit passt in den Satz? Trage es ein.

usually never sometimes always

a) Sheep ______________ sing songs.
b) Children ______________ have to go to school.
c) Fish ______________ swim.
d) It is ______________ very cold in winter.

Adverbiale Orts- und Zeitbestimmungen

Satzteile, die ausdrücken, wo oder wann etwas geschieht, nennt man adverbiale Bestimmungen des Ortes und der Zeit.

Adverbiale Bestimmungen des Ortes	**Adverbiale Bestimmungen der Zeit**
in the garden	on Saturday
at school	in September
on the table	at night
on the beach	from 10 until 4

Adverbiale Bestimmungen stehen im Englischen meist am Ende des Satzes.

I have breakfast at home. I play tennis on Monday. I like to go to school.

Vor allem Zeitangaben können auch am Satzanfang stehen. Die Wortfolge im Satz ändert sich dadurch nicht.

We go to church on Sunday. On Sunday we go to church.

Wenn gleichzeitig eine Ortsbestimmung und eine Zeitbestimmung im Satz vorkommen, erscheint immer der Ort vor der Zeit.

We have breakfast ....at home.......................at 9 o'clock.
Our teachers work...................at school.....................from 8 until 2.
Mother works..........................in the garden...............every day.

1 Was sind Ortsbestimmungen? Was sind Zeitbestimmungen? Sortiere die Begriffe.

at the hospital on the train every February in the country in summer on Tuesday

Adverbiale Bestimmung des Ortes	Adverbiale Bestimmung der Zeit
______________________	______________________
______________________	______________________
______________________	______________________

2 Schreibe die Satzteile in der richtigen Reihenfolge auf. Beachte: Ort vor Zeit!

a) Mum and Dad / in the living room / watch TV / every evening

____

b) go / my grandparents / to bed / never / after midnight

____

c) do my homework / from 4 until 5 / usually / I / at the kitchen table

____

Fragen mit Fragewörtern und Hilfsverben

Viele Fragen werden mit sogenannten Fragewörtern eingeleitet. Wenn das folgende Verb ein Hilfsverb ist (z. B. "to be", "to have" oder "can"), folgt es unmittelbar nach dem Fragewort.

Frage	Englisches Fragewort	Beispiel
nach einer Person (Wer? Wen?)	Who?	Who is that boy? Who can you see at the window?
nach einer Sache (Was? Welche/r/s?)	What?	What are you watching on TV? What colour is your bike?
nach einem Ort (Wo? Wohin?)	Where?	Where is my pencil? Where are you going?
nach einem Zeitpunkt (Wann?)	When?	When can we play together?
nach einer Eigenschaft (Wie?)	How?	How old are you?
nach einer Ursache (Warum?)	Why?	Why can't you come?

1 Frage nach dem hervorgehobenen Wort oder Satzteil, so wie im Beispiel.

a) **Mike** is Sarah's brother. Who is Sarah's brother? ______
b) My school is in **Oxford**. ______
c) Tim is **eleven**. ______
d) My parents are at a party **today**. ______
e) I can see **my father** in the garden. ______
f) We've got a **cake**. ______

2 Setze die passenden Fragewörter ein.

why where when what

a) ______ is your school?
b) ______ are you doing?
c) ______ can you do your homework today?
d) ______ are you so happy?

Das Verb "is" wird im gesprochenen und geschriebenen Englisch oft mit den Fragewörtern zu einer Kurzform zusammengezogen.

Who's Bill? What's your name? Where's my car? When's your birthday?

Fragen mit Fragewörtern und Vollverben

Immer dann, wenn kein Hilfsverb (zum Beispiel “to be”, “to have” oder “can”) vorhanden ist, wird die Frage im Englischen mit einer Form von “to do” gebildet. Verneinte Fragen bildet man entsprechend mit “don’t” oder “doesn’t”.

Bejahte Fragesätze	Verneinte Fragesätze
Who do you meet at the bus station?	Why don’t you play with Dave?
What does Brian do on Mondays?	Who don’t you like?
How do you feel this morning?	When doesn’t he work?

Hier gibt es eine Ausnahme: Die Frage wird ohne “to do” gebildet, wenn mit “who” nach dem Subjekt (Satzgegenstand) gefragt wird, die deutsche Übersetzung von “who” also „wer“ ist.

Who hates flies?	Who makes a terrible noise?	Who goes to school?
Mr Cook hates flies.	Monsters make a terrible noise.	Children go to school.

1 Frage nach dem hervorgehobenen Satzteil, wie im Beispiel.

a) Ann likes **cornflakes**. What does Ann like?
b) The stars shine **at night**. ____________________
c) Our cat usually sits **on the chair**. ____________________
d) My Mum often helps **me**. ____________________

2 Frage nach dem hervorgehobenen Wort. Wird hier “do” oder “does” gebraucht oder nicht? Achte darauf, ob nach dem Satzgegenstand gefragt wird (englisch: “who” = deutsch: „wer“).

a) **Billie** loves cats. ____________________
b) Kathy loves **Ken**. ____________________
c) Ken helps **his father**. ____________________
d) **Sally** helps her mother. ____________________

Im formellen Englisch wird häufig noch das Fragewort “whom” verwendet, wenn man nach dem Objekt fragt (englisch: “whom” = deutsch: „wen“).

Dann steht	“Whom do you meet?”	statt	“Who do you meet?”
	“Whom can I help?”	statt	“Who can I help?”

Entscheidungsfragen

Wenn man Fragen mit Ja oder Nein beantworten kann, nennt man sie Entscheidungsfragen. Sie beginnen mit dem Hilfsverb (zum Beispiel "to be", "to have" oder "can"). Wenn kein Hilfsverb vorhanden ist, beginnen sie mit "do" bzw. "doesn't".

Entscheidungsfragen mit Hilfsverben:

Is Helen English?
Have you got a pencil?
Can you give me a drink?

Entscheidungsfragen bei Vollverben:

Do you speak English?
Does Eric live in Italy?
Do you like to dance?

Verneinte Fragen bildet man entsprechend:

Isn't Charles English?
Haven't you got a rubber?
Can't you see the tree over there?

Don't you come from Berlin?
Doesn't he work in the supermarket?
Doesn't Linda live in Oxford?

1 Bilde aus jedem Satz eine Entscheidungsfrage wie im Beispiel.

a) Eric goes to school. Does he go to school?
b) The children have fun. ______
c) Patty is Douglas' girlfriend. ______
d) Dad reads the newspaper every day. ______
e) Our guests leave at 5 o'clock. ______
f) Keith can come tomorrow. ______
g) The dog is barking. ______

2 Die folgenden Fragen sollst du verneint stellen. Beachte das Beispiel.

a) Bob likes Karen. Doesn't Bob like Karen?
b) Mr Keiton often reads books. ______
c) The mobile phone is ringing. ______
d) He has got a new bike. ______
e) We can do our homework later. ______
f) Mrs Snuggs is very busy today. ______
g) We usually go on holiday in July. ______

Kurzantworten

Im Englischen bejaht man Entscheidungsfragen nicht nur mit “yes”, sondern man formuliert sogenannte Kurzantworten. Dabei wird das Hilfsverb oder die Form von “to do” wiederholt.

Are you twelve? Yes, I am.
Can we play tennis? Yes, we can.
Has he got a new shirt? Yes, he has.
Do you like holidays? Yes, I do.

Auch die verneinende Antwort mit “no” wird meist auf diese Weise ergänzt.

Is she German? No, she isn’t.
Can you play chess? No, I can’t.
Have you got a pet? No, we haven’t.
Does he sleep before midnight? No, he doesn’t.

1 Ergänze “yes” und “no” mit den passenden Kurzantworten.

a) Does he like his parents? Yes, ______________________
b) Are they drinking milk? No, ______________________
c) Have we got the key? No, ______________________
d) Do you like money? Yes, ______________________
e) Is Susan ugly? No, ______________________
f) Can she stay until tomorrow? No, ______________________

2 Beantworte die Fragen zu dem Bild und verwende die Kurzantworten.

a) Do you see a duck in the picture? ______________________
b) Are the boys playing tennis? ______________________
c) Has the man got a bike? ______________________
d) Can you see a woman in the picture? ______________________

Zählbare und nicht zählbare Mengen

Der Artikel wird bei Nomen nur gebraucht, wenn es sich um eine Menge von Dingen handelt, die grundsätzlich zählbar ist. Wenn Nomen im allgemeinen Sinn gebraucht werden und damit eigentlich eine unzählbare Menge gemeint ist, verwendet man sie ohne Artikel.

Mit Artikel	Ohne Artikel
Look at the lions in the zoo.	Lions eat meat.
Can you see the cars over there?	Cars are expensive.

Viele der Nomen für Lebensmittel haben keinen Plural, weil sie Dinge bezeichnen, die man grundsätzlich nicht zählen kann, wie Milch oder Eis. Solche Nomen werden nur dann mit einem Artikel versehen, wenn zum Beispiel eine ganz bestimmte Tüte Milch oder eine einzelne Portion Eis gemeint sind.

salt pepper sugar ice cream milk tea chocolate

I don't like tea with milk.
I like ice cream with chocolate.

Aber: Can you pass me the milk, please? Can I have an ice cream, please?

1 Überlege: Wird der Begriff allgemein gebraucht oder ist eine bestimmte Menge gemeint? Setze dann die Wörter mit oder ohne Artikel ein.

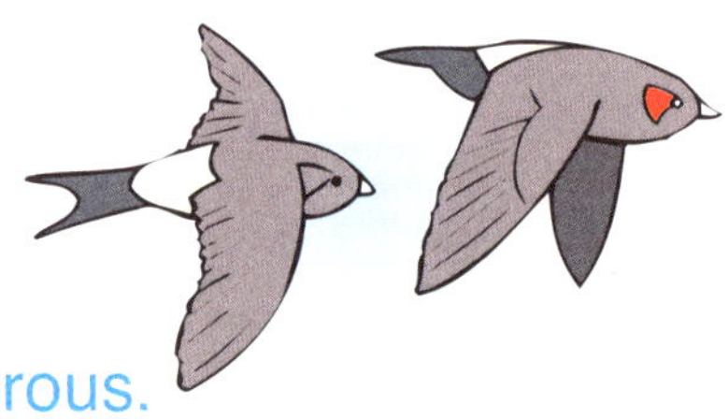

a) ______________ can be dangerous.
b) ______________ in the sky are singing.
c) ______________ usually hate ______________.
d) ______________ in our garden are beautiful.
e) Do you like ______________ with ______________?

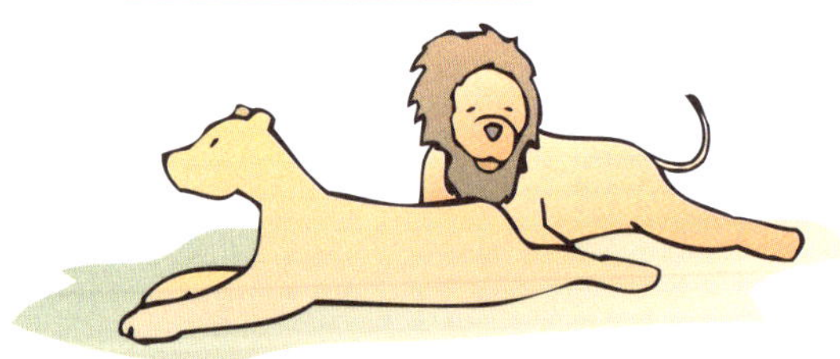

2 Kreuze den einzigen Satz an, der zu dem Bild passt.

a) English people drink a lot of tea.
b) Carol likes to drink milk.
c) The milkman brings the milk every morning.
d) Carol likes to drink tea.

"much" und "many"

Für das deutsche Wort „viel" gibt es im Englischen zwei Begriffe. Das Wort "much" wird verwendet, wenn es sich um nicht zählbare Nomen handelt. Dagegen sagt man bei zählbaren Nomen "many".

Nicht zählbare Nomen

How much coffee is in the pot?
How much money have you got?

Zählbare Nomen

How many sisters has Bill got?
How many cakes are in the box?

Bei Fragen wird fast immer "much" oder "many" gebraucht. Das gilt auch für verneinte Aussagesätze. Bei bejahten Aussagesätzen steht dagegen oft "a lot of" oder "lots of". Damit kann man sowohl "much" wie auch "many" ersetzen.

Verneinte Aussagesätze

Diana hasn't got much bread.
I don't know many people.

Bejahte Aussagesätze

Charles has got lots of friends.
He has got a lot of time.

1 Hier sind Fragen und verneinte Aussagesätze. Setze "much" oder "many" richtig ein.

a) How __________ butter is in the fridge?
b) How __________ trees are in your garden?
c) I cannot eat __________ meat.
d) Mrs Hill usually doesn't buy __________ apples.
e) How __________ books have you got?

2 Hier findest du außer Fragen und verneinten Aussagesätzen auch bejahte Aussagesätze, bei denen du "a lot of" oder "lots of" verwenden kannst.

a) How __________ milk is in the bottle?
b) I like to eat __________ ice cream.
c) Look – there are __________ clouds in the sky.
d) There are __________ flies in the kitchen.
e) Mariah doesn't like __________ tea.

Mit "how much" fragt man im Englischen nach dem Preis einer Ware.

How much is the guitar?
It's 50 pounds.

How much are the books?
They are 10 pounds.

"some" und "any" in Aussagesätzen

Das englische Wort "some" hat im Deutschen die Bedeutung „einige, ein paar". Es wird bei bejahten Aussagesätzen gebraucht. "Any" verwendet man dagegen bei verneinten Aussagesätzen.

Bejahte Aussagesätze

I've got some books.
There are some children in the schoolyard.

Verneinte Aussagesätze

I haven't got any books.
There aren't any teachers.

"Some" und "any" können auch vor unzählbaren Nomen stehen.

I need some milk.

I don't need any sugar.

1 Entscheide, ob du "some" oder "any" einsetzen musst.

a) There are ____________ newspapers on the table.
b) There isn't ____________ soap in the bathroom.
c) There are ____________ cherries on the tree.
d) There aren't ____________ eggs in the nest.
e) We haven't got ____________ butter.

2 Was Bill hat, hat Sarah nicht – und umgekehrt. Schreibe jeweils den zweiten Satz.

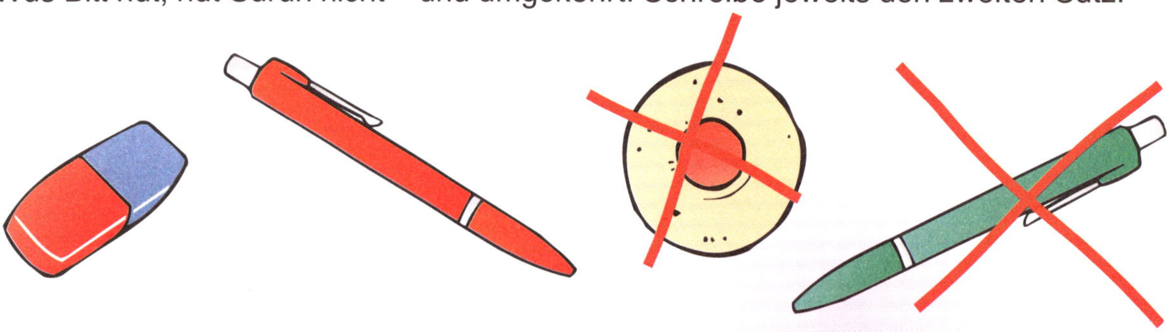

a) Bill has got ________________________ rubbers.
Sarah ______________________________ rubbers.

b) Bill hasn't got ________ biros.
Sarah ______________________________ biros.

c) Bill has got __________ cookies.
Sarah ______________________________ cookies.

d) Bill hasn't got _______ chocolate.
Sarah ______________________________ chocolate.

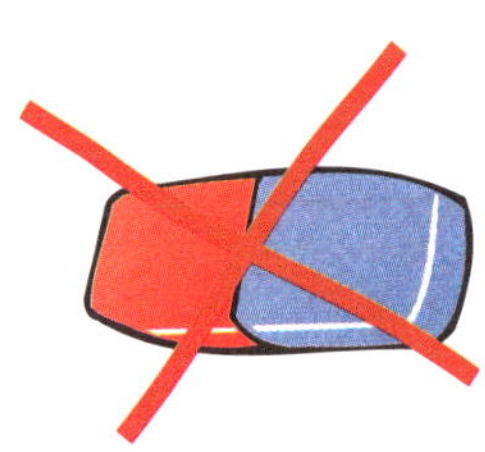

e) Bill doesn't drink ________ milk.
Sarah usually ______________________ milk.

"some" und "any" bei Fragen und Antworten

Wenn man bei einer Frage die Antwort wirklich nicht weiß, nennt man das eine offene Frage. Bei solchen Fragen wird in den meisten Fällen "any" verwendet. In der Antwort erscheint "some" oder "any" – je nachdem, ob die Frage bejaht oder verneint wird. Das Nomen wird dabei oft nicht wiederholt.

Frage	Bejahte Antwort	Verneinte Antwort
Does she read any books?	Yes, she reads some.	No, she doesn't read any.
Do you like any animals?	Yes, I like some.	No, I don't like any.

Wenn man allerdings von vornherein eine bejahende Antwort erwartet, dann wird auch in Fragen "some" verwendet – zum Beispiel, wenn man jemandem etwas anbietet.

Do you want to have some biscuits?
Do you want to read some books?
Do you want to have some coffee?

1 Überlege, ob es sich um eine offene Frage handelt oder ob eine bejahende Antwort erwartet wird. Setze "any" und "some" richtig ein.

a) Are there ________ people in the church?
b) Do you want to have ________ tea?
c) Are there ________ children at the playground?
d) Are there ________ tourists in the museum?
e) Do you want to have ________ ice cream?
f) Are there ________ eggs in the fridge?

Es gibt einige zusammengesetzte Wörter, für die dieselben Anwendungsregeln wie für "some" und "any" gelten.

someone – anyone (jemand)
somewhere – anywhere (irgendwo)
something – anything (etwas)

Someone is knocking at the door.
Is there anyone at school today?
Mum is somewhere in the house.
Dave cannot find his rubber anywhere.

Do you see anything behind the curtain?
I can hear something under my bed.

Adjektive

Wenn man ein Nomen genauer beschreiben möchte, gebraucht man ein Adjektiv.

an apple — a **green** apple
a woman — a **nice** woman
a dog — a **dangerous** dog

Adjektive stehen meist vor dem Nomen, so wie in den Beispielen oben. Sie können aber auch nach einer Form von "to be" folgen. Dann beschreibt der ganze Satz, wie etwas ist.

The boy is tall. He's a tall boy.
The car is slow. It's a slow car.
The cows are white and brown. They're white and brown cows.

Wenn die Eigenschaft, die das Adjektiv beschreibt, besonders stark ausgeprägt ist, kann man das Wort "very" davorsetzen.

He's a very funny clown. Look, there's a very old man.

1 Verwende die Adjektive wie im Beispiel.

a) bike / red The bike is red. It's a red bike.
b) girl / young ______
c) noise / terrible ______
d) children / happy ______
e) woman / beautiful ______
f) sky / blue ______

2 Unterstreiche die Adjektive in den folgenden Sätzen. Pass auf! Ein Satz enthält zwei Adjektive, ein Satz enthält gar kein Adjektiv.

a) Usually Paul is very hungry.
b) Our lazy cat usually lies under the old tree in our garden.
c) The TV programme wasn't funny yesterday.
d) The girls and boys are singing and dancing.
e) Peggy has got a new pencil.

Ausrufe mit "how" und "what"

Wenn man Überraschung, Enttäuschung, Erstaunen oder Bewunderung durch einen Ausruf ausdrückt, verwendet man dabei meist ein Adjektiv.

How interesting! How funny! How nice!

Ergänzt man bei solchen Ausrufen auch noch das Nomen, dann muss man die richtige Wortfolge sehr genau einhalten, sonst wird eine Frage daraus.

Ausruf	Frage	Ausruf	Frage
How fast your car is!	How fast is your car?	How clever you are!	How clever are you?

In ähnlicher Weise können Ausrufe auch mit "what" formuliert werden.

What a nice cat! What a pretty dress!

Der unbestimmte Artikel "a / an" wird dabei nur verwendet, wenn es sich um ein zählbares Nomen handelt (a cat, a woman, a dress ...). Unzählbare Nomen (milk, sugar, tea ...) sowie Nomen im Plural erscheinen in solchen Ausrufen ohne Artikel.

What smelly cheese! What beautiful roses!

1 Zu jedem Bild passen zwei Ausrufe.
Schreibe die entsprechenden Buchstaben in die Kreise.

a) What a long nose you've got!
b) What a horrible animal!
c) How nice your baby is!
d) What noisy boys!
e) How long your nose is!
f) How horrible this animal is!
g) How noisy the boys are!
h) What a nice baby!

Die Steigerung von Adjektiven

Wenn man verschiedene Dinge in ihrer jeweiligen Eigenschaft miteinander vergleichen will, gebraucht man die Steigerungsformen des Adjektivs. Sie heißen Komparativ und Superlativ.

Grundform	**Komparativ**	**Superlativ**
klein	kleiner	am kleinsten
dunkel	dunkler	am dunkelsten
langsam	langsamer	am langsamsten

Im Englischen wird bei einsilbigen Adjektiven der Komparativ durch das Anhängen von -er gebildet. Der Superlativ entsteht durch das Anhängen von -est.

Grundform	**Komparativ**	**Superlativ**
small	small**er**	small**est**
dark	dark**er**	dark**est**
slow	slow**er**	slow**est**

1 Steigere die folgenden Adjektive wie im Beispiel.

Grundform	Komparativ	Superlativ
a) old	older	oldest
b) young	________	________
c) fast	________	________
d) deep	________	________
e) tall	________	________
f) cheap	________	________
g) bright	________	________
h) warm	________	________

2 Du siehst die Bärenmutter mit ihren Jungen beim Weitsprung (long jump).
Schreibe das Adjektiv "long" und seine Steigerungsformen richtig unter die Bären.

a) ________ b) ________ c) ________

Besondere Schreibweisen bei der Steigerung von Adjektiven

Bei einigen der einsilbigen Adjektive muss man bei der Steigerung Besonderheiten in der Schreibweise beachten.
Bei Adjektiven, die auf -e enden, fällt dieses -e beim Komparativ und Superlativ weg.

Grundform	Komparativ	Superlativ
late	lat**er**	lat**est**
fine	fin**er**	fin**est**

Wenn auf einen einzelnen betonten Vokal ein einzelner Endkonsonant folgt, wird dieser Konsonant in den Steigerungsformen verdoppelt.

Grundform	Komparativ	Superlativ
big	big**ger**	big**gest**
sad	sad**der**	sad**dest**

Auch zweisilbige Adjektive, die auf -y enden, werden mit -er und -est gesteigert. Das -y verwandelt sich dabei in ein -i.

Grundform	Komparativ	Superlativ
easy	eas**ier**	eas**iest**
pretty	prett**ier**	prett**iest**

1 Steigere diese Adjektive und beachte dabei die besonderen Schreibweisen.

Grundform	Komparativ	Superlativ
a) nice	______	______
b) happy	______	______
c) hot	______	______
d) dirty	______	______
e) small	______	______
f) angry	______	______
g) heavy	______	______
h) funny	______	______

2 Ordne dem Adjektiv "hot" und seinen Steigerungsformen die richtigen Bilder zu.

a) ______

b) ______

c) ______

Die Steigerung mit "more" und "most"

Die meisten mehrsilbigen Adjektive werden gesteigert, indem man ihnen im Komparativ "more" und im Superlativ "most" voranstellt.

Grundform	Komparativ	Superlativ
intelligent	**more** intelligent	**most** intelligent
nervous	**more** nervous	**most** nervous

1 Unterstreiche nur die Adjektive, die mit "more" und "most" gesteigert werden.

expensive	quick	old	tired	happy	deep
fast	aggressive	exciting	young	careful	slow
dirty	boring	marvellous	terrible	difficult	fine

2 Überprüfe im Lösungsteil, ob du alle Adjektive in Aufgabe 1 gefunden hast. Schreibe sie nun auf und steigere sie.

	Grundform	Komparativ	Superlativ
a)	expensive	more	most
b)			
c)			
d)			
e)			
f)			
g)			
h)			
i)			

3 Lauter Rekorde! Schreibe jeweils den passenden Superlativ mit "most" unter das Bild.

expensive
terrible
intelligent

a) ____________

b) ____________

c) ____________

Verschiedene Steigerungen im Vergleich

Weil sich die Steigerung von Adjektiven im Englischen teilweise vom Deutschen unterscheidet, ist es wichtig, darauf zu achten, wann man die verschiedenen Steigerungsarten verwendet.

Steigerung mit -er und -est

- alle einsilbigen Adjektive
- zweisilbige Adjektive, die auf -y enden

Steigerung mit more und most

- zweisilbige Adjektive, die nicht auf -y enden
- alle Adjektive mit mehr als zwei Silben

1 Hier stehen jeweils vier Grundformen, vier Komparative und vier Superlative durcheinander. Trage die Adjektive in die richtige Spalte der Tabelle ein.

sweet happier most difficult sweeter more difficult sweetest happiest difficult beautiful happy more beautiful most beautiful

Grundformen	Komparative	Superlative
______	______	______
______	______	______
______	______	______
______	______	______

2 Hier stehen Adjektive aus beiden Steigerungsarten. Entscheide, welche Steigerungsart du verwenden musst.

Grundform	Komparativ	Superlativ
a) tall	______	______
b) silly	______	______
c) marvellous	______	______
d) new	______	______
e) nervous	______	______
f) great	______	______
g) high	______	______
h) happy	______	______

Drei Adjektive haben Steigerungsformen, die von allen Regeln abweichen. Man sollte sie sich gut merken.

Grundform	**Komparativ**	**Superlativ**
good	better	best
bad	worse	worst
far	farther/further	farthest/furthest

Das Vergleichen von Eigenschaften

Um in einem Satz auszudrücken, dass sich Dinge oder Personen in einer Eigenschaft unterscheiden, wird das Wort "than" benutzt.

Is Ben shorter or taller **than** Tim? .... Ben is shorter **than** Tim.
Is Mum younger or older **than** Dad? .... Mum is younger **than** Dad.

Wenn man ausdrücken möchte, dass Dinge oder Personen gleiche Eigenschaften haben, verwendet man "as ... as".

My dog is **as** nice **as** your dog.
Our car is **as** fast **as** Smiths' car.

Personalpronomen stehen anders als im Deutschen nach "than" bzw. "as ...as" in der Objektform (me, him, her, us, them).

Ben ist größer als **ich**. – Ben is taller than **me**.
Ich bin intelligenter als **er**. – I'm more intelligent than **him**.

1 Schau dir das Bild an. Schreibe dann vergleichende Sätze mit den angegebenen Wörtern wie im Beispiel.

a) (Tom / tall / Ann) Tom is taller than Ann.

b) (Ann's hair / long / Tom's hair)

____

c) (Tom's hair / dark / Ann's hair)

____

d) (Tom's bag / big / Ann's bag)

____

e) (Ann's bag / small / Tom's bag)

____

2 Schreibe den Satz auf und verwende Personalpronomen wie im Beispiel.

a) Bill is as tall as his friend.
Bill says: "I'm as tall as him."

b) Susan is older than her sister.
Susan says: "I'm ________________________."

c) Mike is as funny as Nick.
Mike says: "I'm ________________________."

d) The Millers are as rich as the Smiths.
The Millers say: "The Smiths are ________________."

e) Kate is older than her brother.
Kate says: "My brother is __________________."

Wenn man einen Vergleich verneint ausdrücken will, hat man zwei Möglichkeiten.
Man kann den Ausdruck "not as ... as" (nicht so ... wie) verwenden.

The weather is **not as** fine **as** yesterday.
The football game was **not as** good **as** yesterday.

Man kann auch "less ... than" (weniger ... als) sagen.

Sally's dress is **less** beautiful **than** Linda's dress.
I'm **less** nervous **than** you.

1 Kate findet sich klein und hässlich. Sie vergleicht sich mit Mary. Schreibe Sätze wie im Beispiel auf. Verwende entweder "not as ... as" oder "less ... than".

a) (tall) I'm not as tall as Mary.
b) (long) My hair ______________________ Mary's hair.
c) (beautiful) I'm ______________________ Mary.
d) (slim) My legs ______________________ Mary's legs.
e) (intelligent) I'm ______________________ Mary.
f) (funny) I'm ______________________ Mary.
g) (fantastic) My voice ______________________ Mary's voice.
h) (bright) My eyes ______________________ Mary's eyes.
i) (attractive) I'm ______________________ Mary.

2 Vergleiche die Preise. Verwende alle Steigerungsformen, die du gelernt hast.

a) (expensive) The trousers are ______________________ the hat.
b) (cheap) The hat is ______________________ the shirt.
c) (cheap) The socks are ______________________ the hat.
d) (expensive) The shirt is ______________________ the trousers.
e) (expensive) The shirt is ______________________ the hat.
f) (cheap) The hat is ______________________ the trousers.

Adverbien der Art und Weise

Mit Adverbien der Art und Weise wird näher beschrieben, wie eine Tätigkeit ausgeführt wird. Die meisten Adverbien werden gebildet, indem man die Endsilbe -ly an ein Adjektiv hängt.

Adjektiv	Adverb
slow	slow**ly**
quick	quick**ly**
dangerous	dangerous**ly**

Im Deutschen haben Adjektive und Adverbien die gleiche Form, im Englischen jedoch nicht. Daher muss man sehr genau auf den Unterschied in der Verwendung von Adjektiven und Adverbien achten.

Ein Adjektiv beschreibt, wie eine Sache oder eine Person ist.	Ein Adverb beschreibt, wie eine Tätigkeit ausgeführt wird.
Mr Clark is a **quick driver**.	Today Mr Clark isn't **driving quickly**.
Diana was very **sad** yesterday.	She was **crying sadly**.
Hugh is a **careful boy**.	He is **carefully riding** his bike.

1 Verwandle die Adjektive in Adverbien.

a) careful ______________ b) loud ______________
c) great ______________ d) bad ______________
e) nervous ______________ f) tender ______________

2 Adjektiv oder Adverb? Überlege gut und setze jeweils das richtige Wort ein.

quick quickly

a) Aunt Millie has got a very ______________ car.
b) Ken is doing the shopping very ______________ .

dangerous dangerously

c) A crocodile is a ______________ animal.
d) A drunken person usually drives ______________ .

bright brightly

e) The sun shines ______________ .
f) Susan likes ______________ colours.

Besondere Schreibweisen bei Adverbien

Bei einigen Adverbien muss man auf ihre besondere Schreibweise achten.
So wird das -y eines Adjektivs zum -i, wenn die Adverb-Endung -ly angehängt wird.

Adjektiv	Adverb
happy	happ**ily**
angry	angr**ily**

Bei Adjektiven, die auf -le enden, fällt diese Endung vollständig weg, wenn die Adverb-Endung -ly angehängt wird.

Adjektiv	Adverb
terrible	terri**bly**
horrible	horri**bly**

Endet ein Adjektiv auf -ic, dann wird beim Adverb die Form -ally angehängt.

Adjektiv	Adverb
automatic	automatic**ally**
basic	basic**ally**

Bei einigen Wörtern haben Adjektiv und Adverb völlig gleiche Formen.

hard	My uncle is a hard worker.	My uncle works very hard.
fast	I've got a fast car.	I can drive fast with my new car.
long	We waited for a long time.	I don't like to wait long.
early	Tom rises at an early hour.	He always rises early.
weekly	I read the weekly magazine.	I read it weekly.
daily	Everybody has got daily duties.	You have to brush your teeth daily.

Und noch eine Ausnahme: Das Adverb zu "good" heißt "well".

Ben is a good tennis player. He plays tennis well.

1 Schreibe zu jedem Adjektiv das dazugehörende Adverb. Beachte alle Regeln und Ausnahmen, die auf dieser Seite beschrieben werden.

a) easy ____________ b) fantastic ____________
c) early ____________ d) pretty ____________
e) good ____________ f) electronic ____________
g) terrible ____________ h) daily ____________
i) hard ____________ j) long ____________

2 Schreibe jeweils auf, ob das unterstrichene Wort hier ein Adjektiv oder ein Adverb ist.

a) I usually get up <u>early</u> in the morning. ____________
b) The <u>early</u> bird catches the worm. ____________
c) You've got a <u>long</u> nose. ____________
d) I usually don't wait <u>long</u> at the bus stop. ____________

Steigerung von Adverbien

Alle Adverbien, die auf -ly enden, werden mit “more / most” gesteigert.

Sam paints fantastically.	Ken paints **more** fantastically.	Robbie paints **most** fantastically.

Die einsilbigen Adverbien werden mit -er / -est gesteigert.

Sheila runs fast.	Rickie runs fast**er**.	Clara runs fast**est**.

Die beiden Adverbien “well” und “badly” haben eigene Steigerungsformen.

well	better	best
badly	worse	worst

1 Immer mehr und mehr … Steigere die Adverbien wie im Beispiel.

a) (to work hard) Mr Smith works hard.
Mr Miller works harder.
Mr Baker works hardest.

b) (to shout angrily) Dad ______________________
Grandpa ______________________
Mum ______________________

c) (to sing terribly) Kim ______________________
Mary ______________________
Ronald ______________________

d) (to play the guitar well) Cindy ______________________
Dave ______________________
Brian ______________________

e) (to do his homework badly) Fred ______________________
Frank ______________________
John ______________________

Adverbien im Vergleich

Wenn Adverbien miteinander verglichen werden, gelten die gleichen Regeln wie bei Adjektiven. Es werden die Wörter "than", "as ... as" , "not as … as" und "less … than" gebraucht.

I can run **as** fast **as** Mary.
But I can run faster **than** Bob.
Bob can't run **as** fast **as** me.

I cried terribly last night.
I cried **as** terribly **as** you.
I think I cried **more** terribly **than** you.
Perhaps I cried **less** terribly **than** you.

1 Olympiade der kleinen Tiere: Wer ist der Schnellste? Schreibe die entsprechenden Vergleiche mit dem Adverb "fast" und verwende "faster ... than", "as ... as" und "not as ... as".

a) (spider – earthworm) The spider runs faster than the earthworm.
b) (earthworm – snail) ______
c) (spider – ant) ______
d) (snail – caterpillar) ______
e) (earthworm – ant) ______
f) (caterpillar – earthworm) ______

2 Vergleiche nun die Sieger der Kleintier-Olympiade mit dem Adverb "slowly". Verwende "more … than", "as ... as", "less … than".

a) (snail – ant) The snail crawls more slowly than the ant.
b) (earthworm – caterpillar) ______
c) (earthworm – spider) ______
d) (spider – ant) ______
e) (earthworm – snail) ______
f) (spider – snail) ______

Die einfache Gegenwart - simple present

Bei der Zeitform der einfachen Gegenwart (simple present) entsprechen fast alle Formen dem Infinitiv des Verbs. In der 3. Person Singular wird jedoch an den Infinitiv noch ein -s angehängt.

to sing	to dream	to shout
I sing	I dream	I shout
you sing	you dream	you shout
he sing**s**	Jim dream**s**	Mr Keiton shout**s**
she sing**s**	Sally dream**s**	Mrs Smith shout**s**
it sing**s**	the cat dream**s**	the parrot shout**s**
we sing	we dream	we shout
you sing	you dream	you shout
they sing	the boys and girls dream	the people shout

Die einfache Gegenwart wird immer dann verwendet, wenn eine Handlung immer, regelmäßig oder niemals stattfindet. Einige Wörter weisen darauf hin, dass man die einfache Gegenwart verwenden muss, zum Beispiel:

always (immer)	sometimes (manchmal)	often (oft, häufig)
usually (normalerweise)	seldom, rarely (selten)	never (niemals)

1 Entscheide, ob hier jeweils in der einfachen Gegenwart ein -s angehängt wird oder nicht.

a) (run) he ________________
b) (laugh) Sam ________________
c) (whisper) we ________________
d) (shine) it ________________
e) (phone) they ________________
f) (wait) you ________________

2 Setze in die folgenden Sätze das Verb in der einfachen Gegenwart ein. Achte darauf, ob du ein -s anhängen musst. Gebrauche die angegebenen Verben.

wait   love   hate   sleep   sing

a) Billy ________________ to do his homework.
b) We often ________________ before midnight.
c) Pat ________________ animals.
d) The birds usually ________________ in the morning.
e) Ronald often ________________ at the bus stop.

Wichtige Hilfsverben

Die Verben “to be”, “to have” und “to do” werden im Englischen immer wieder gebraucht, um verschiedene Zeitformen zu bilden oder um Fragen und Verneinungen zu formulieren. Man nennt sie in diesem Zusammenhang Hilfsverben. Bei “to be” und “to have” werden sowohl im gesprochenen wie auch im schriftlichen Englisch häufig Kurzformen verwendet. Sie stehen hier hinter dem Schrägstrich.

to be	to have	to do
I am / I'm	I have / I've	I do
you are / you're	you have / you've	you do
he is / he's	he has / he's	he does
she is / she's	she has / she's	she does
it is / it's	it has / it's	it does
we are / we're	we have / we've	we do
you are / you're	you have / you've	you do
they are / they're	they have / they've	they do

Alle drei Verben werden durch das Anhängen von “not” verneint. Auch dabei gibt es Kurzformen, die nahezu immer verwendet werden.

I am not / I'm not	I have not / I haven't	I do not / I don't
you are not / you aren't	you have not / you haven't	you do not / you don't
he is not / he isn't	he has not / he hasn't	he does not / he doesn't
she is not / she isn't	she has not / she hasn't	she does not / she doesn't
it is not / it isn't	it has not / it hasn't	it does not / it doesn't
we are not / we aren't	we have not / we haven't	we do not / we don't
you are not / you aren't	you have not / you haven't	you do not / you don't
they are not / they aren't	they have not / they haven't	they do not / they don't

1 Schreibe das Verb erst in der Langform auf. Schreibe die Kurzform dahinter.

… to be …
a) he is / he's

… to be …
b) we ____________

… to be …
c) it ____________

… to have …
d) you ____________

… to have …
e) they ____________

… to have …
f) she ____________

2 Schreibe jeweils die verneinte Form wie im Beispiel auf.

a) I do / I don't
b) he has / ____________
c) we are / ____________
d) it does / ____________
e) they have / ____________
f) she is / ____________

Die Verlaufsform der Gegenwart - present progressive

Wenn im Englischen Handlungen beschrieben werden, die gerade stattfinden und noch nicht beendet sind, verwendet man die Verlaufsform der Gegenwart (present progressive). Sie wird aus "to be" und der sogenannten -ing-Form des Verbs gebildet.

I **am** repair**ing** my bike.

My father **is** work**ing** in the garden.

Dabei kann auch die Kurzform von "to be" verwendet werden.

We'**re** play**ing** tennis.

She'**s** read**ing** a book.

Manche Verben verändern sich etwas, wenn man die -ing-Form bildet.

Bei Verben mit einem -e am Ende, das nicht mitgesprochen wird, verschwindet dieses -e bei der -ing-Form.

to drive – he's driving
to come – we're coming
to write – she's writing

Wenn ein kurz gesprochener und betonter Selbstlaut (a, e, i, o, u) vor einem einfachen Mitlaut am Ende des Infinitivs steht, wird dieser Mitlaut bei der -ing-Form verdoppelt.

to sit – I'm sitting
to stop – he's stopping
to begin – we're beginning

1 Schreibe Sätze in der Verlaufsform. Verwende die angegebenen Nomen, Personalpronomen und Verben. Du kannst entweder die Kurzform (I'm, you're, he's ...) oder die Langform verwenden.

a) (The cat – sleep) ______________________
b) (Mary – sing) ______________________
c) (You – jump) ______________________
d) (The football players – shout) ______________________
e) (We – work in the garden) ______________________
f) (I – do my homework) ______________________

2 Bilde von den folgenden Verben die -ing-Form. Beachte die Ausnahmeregeln.

a) to make ____________ b) to put ____________
c) to listen ____________ d) to write ____________
e) to run ____________ f) to rain ____________
g) to dance ____________ h) to shop ____________
i) to go ____________ j) to swim ____________

Einfache Gegenwart und Verlaufsform im Vergleich

Da es im Deutschen nur eine Gegenwartsform gibt, muss man besonders darauf achten, wie im Englischen die einfache Gegenwart und die Verlaufsform unterschieden werden.

Verlaufsform
Passiert etwas gerade jetzt?

It's raining today.
I'm making some tea.

Einfache Gegenwart
Passiert etwas immer, selten oder nie?

My father never drinks tea at breakfast.
He always drinks coffee.

1 Entscheide, ob du die Verlaufsform oder die einfache Gegenwart verwenden musst.

a) Be quiet. I ____________________ to the radio. (to listen)
b) It usually ____________________ in Scotland. (to rain)
c) Danny ____________________ a letter to his dad now. (to write)
d) Mrs Diver always ____________________ the shopping on Friday. (to do)
e) Look, the man over there ____________________ in the street. (to dance)

2 Kreuze den Satz an, der jeweils zum Bild passt.

a) We are playing tennis.
We usually play tennis on Saturday.

b) Alice is doing the shopping now.
Alice usually does the shopping on Wednesday.

Verneinte Sätze

Im Englischen werden Sätze mit Hilfsverben verneint, indem man “not” ergänzt.

Susan is **not** doing her homework.
We have **not** got any money.
Cedric may **not** go to the cinema.
You must **not** park here.
I can**not** speak Russian.

Weil die Verlaufsform der Gegenwart mit dem Hilfsverb “to be” gebildet wird, werden Sätze in dieser Zeitform also auch mit “not” verneint.

I'm **not** playing now, I'm singing.
I'm **not** talking, I'm listening.

Um Sätze in der einfachen Gegenwart zu verneinen, braucht man das Hilfsverb “to do”. Dann wird “do not” / “don't” bzw. “does not” / “doesn't” vor das Verb gesetzt.

Mr Green **doesn't** hate cats.
She **doesn't** leave London.
I **don't** like meat.

1 Schreibe jeweils einen verneinten Satz, indem du “don't” oder “doesn't” verwendest, so wie im Beispiel.

a) My brother plays football. I don't play football.
b) My father reads newspapers. You ______
c) Our dog sleeps in its basket. Our cat ______
d) I like ice cream. My sister ______
e) My mother plays the piano. My father ______
f) The children play chess. Their parents ______

2 Schreibe verneinte Sätze wie im Beispiel. Achte darauf, ob du mit “don't” bzw. “doesn't” verneinen musst oder ob du “not” verwenden kannst.

a) I'm going to school. You aren't going to school.
b) Children usually go to school. Adults ______
c) Eve can go to school by bus. Fred ______
d) We have got a TV. The Millers ______
e) We often go to the theatre. You ______
f) I like our teachers. You ______

Fragen

Es gibt Fragen, die mit einem Fragewort gestellt werden, und Entscheidungsfragen, auf die man mit „ja“ oder „nein“ antworten kann. Grundsätzlich gilt die Regel: Eine Frage wird mit einem Hilfsverb gebildet. Wenn jedoch kein anderes Hilfsverb vorhanden ist, gebraucht man “do” bzw. “does”.

Fragen mit Fragewörtern		Entscheidungsfragen
	mit Hilfsverben	
Who is that girl?		Is she a nice girl?
What are you looking for?		Have you got a new bike?
Where is my mobile phone?		May I use your mobile phone?
When can we watch TV?		Can I watch TV now?
	mit “to do”	
Who do you meet at the bus stop?		Do you meet your best friend?
What does Alex play every Monday?		Does he play chess every Monday?
Where do they go on Sundays?		Do they go to the zoo on Sundays?

Bei verneinten Fragen gilt dasselbe: Entweder wird mit einem Hilfsverb + “not” verneint oder mit “don’t” bzw. “doesn’t”.

Why don’t you like her?
Don’t you come from Hamburg?
Aren’t you German?

1 Setze jeweils das passende Fragewort ein.

what who why where how

a) ______________ is my pencil?
b) ______________ old are you?
c) ______________ colour is your schoolbag?
d) ______________ can you see at the window?
e) ______________ don’t you do your homework?

2 Stelle jeweils eine Entscheidungsfrage wie im Beispiel.

a) The coffee is very hot. Is the coffee very hot?
b) Debbie’s pencil is blue. ______________?
c) John plays football every Monday. ______________?
d) We can go to the zoo on Sunday. ______________?

Wenn das Fragewort “who” nach dem Subjekt des Satzes fragt, wird ausnahmsweise nicht mit “to do” umschrieben!

Who likes hamburgers? Who hates fish and chips?

Das Futur mit "going to"

Wenn man im Englischen über etwas spricht, was man in der Zukunft plant oder beabsichtigt, dann verwendet man eine besondere Zeitform: das Futur mit "going to". Es wird mit einer Form von "to be" gebildet. Dabei wird oft die Kurzform verwendet.

I'**m going to** swim.
You'**re going to** have a shower.
She'**s going to** paint the room.
We'**re going to** eat hamburgers.
You'**re going to** do your homework.
They'**re going to** drive.

Das going-to-Futur wird auch verwendet, wenn ein Ereignis unmittelbar bevorsteht oder wenn es klar vorherzusehen ist.

The football match is going to start.
Mr Miller is going to get wet.

Das going-to-Futur wird verneint, indem an die Form von "to be" ein "not" angehängt wird – normalerweise in der Kurzform.

I'm not going to play with you.
You aren't going to go to the theatre.
It isn't going to rain.
We aren't going to do the shopping.
You aren't going to feed the pets.
They aren't going to wash their car.

1 Schreibe unter jedes Bild einen Satz mit dem going-to-Futur.

to catch a cat · to buy tickets · to play computer games · to buy a new car

a) Simon ______________________

b) The children ______________________

c) The dog ______________________

d) We ______________________

2 Schreibe verneinte Sätze wie im Beispiel auf.

a) We are going to have a drink. You aren't going to have a drink.
b) You're going to have English lessons. I ______________________
c) Willy is going to eat ice cream. David ______________________

Fragen beim Futur mit "going to"

Genau wie bei der Verlaufsform der Gegenwart werden beim going-to-Futur Fragen gestellt, indem Subjekt und Prädikat des Satzes ihren Platz tauschen.

What are we going to do now?
When is he going to play the piano?
Who is Mrs Smith going to meet?
Where is Tim going to go?

Wenn das Fragewort "who" die deutsche Bedeutung "wer" hat, ersetzt es das Subjekt:

Who is going to open the window?
Who is going to visit us?

Auf Entscheidungsfragen wird dabei nicht nur mit "yes" oder "no" geantwortet. Zusätzlich wird das Personalpronomen und die Form von "to be" wiederholt.

Are you going to sleep? .... Yes, I am.
Is Ben going to climb up the wall? .... No, he isn't.
Are the boys going to play football? .... Yes, they are.

1 Stelle Fragen nach dem unterstrichenen Satzteil wie im Beispiel.

a) Ken is going to eat an orange. What is Ken going to eat?
b) Kitty is going to drink milk. __________
c) Mr Green is going to go to Scotland. __________
d) My uncle is going to come at the weekend. __________
e) The plane is going to take off. __________
f) I'm going to meet my uncle. __________

2 Schreibe die Antwort in der entsprechenden Kurzform wie im Beispiel.

a) Is Harry going to play chess? Yes, he is.
b) Are we going to fly to London? No, __________
c) Are they going to have breakfast? Yes, __________
d) Are you going to have a bath? Yes, I __________
e) Is this horse going to run? No, __________
f) Are you going to eat a banana? No, I __________

Das Futur mit "will"

Wenn man über Dinge spricht, die in der Zukunft passieren werden, ohne dass man darauf einen Einfluss hat, verwendet man im Englischen das Futur mit "will".

My father will be fifty in October. The holidays will begin in July.

Zusammen mit Personalpronomen wird nahezu immer eine Kurzform verwendet.

I'll see
you'll see
he'll / she'll / it'll see   my friends at school
we'll see
you'll see
they'll see

Das will-Futur wird auch dann verwendet, wenn man vermutet, dass in der Zukunft etwas geschehen wird. Dabei tauchen oft die Ausdrücke "I think", "I'm sure" oder "maybe" auf.

I think I'll get lots of money for my guitar.
I'm sure my mother will be pleased with your birthday present.
Maybe we'll spend our holidays in Italy next summer.

1 Schreibe den Satz mit dem passenden Personalpronomen wie im Beispiel auf.

a) Mr Douglas will retire next year. He'll retire next year.
b) My sister will have a baby in May. ____________________
c) The Millers will move to London. ____________________
d) The sun will shine tomorrow. ____________________

2 Verwende die vorgegebenen Wörter, um einen Satz mit dem will-Futur zu schreiben.

a) Jenny / twelve / to be / in August Jenny will be twelve in August.
b) I think / to win / England / next time / the football championship

____

c) I'm sure / at the party / have fun / we

____

"will" bedeutet im Englischen immer „werden". Das deutsche „wollen" muss dagegen immer mit "to want to" übersetzt werden.

I want to have a new bike. I want to go home now.

Verneinung und Fragen beim Futur mit "will"

Bei der Verneinung im will-Futur wird statt "will not" fast ausschließlich die Kurzform "won't" verwendet.

I won't meet	
you won't meet	
he / she / it won't meet	the President of the United States
we won't meet	
you won't meet	
they won't meet	

Fragen mit Fragewörtern werden im Futur mit "will" folgendermaßen gebildet:

When will it rain? Where will the football game take place? Who will be the winner?

Beachte: In den Kurzantworten bei Entscheidungsfragen wird das Personalpronomen und die entsprechende Form von "will" wiederholt.

Will he see his teachers? Yes, he will.
Will you care for our parrot? No, I won't.
Will they meet their uncle? No, they won't.

1 Schreibe verneinte Sätze wie im Beispiel.

a) Your father will work in Ireland. My father won't work in Ireland.
b) I'll enjoy your party. Ann ______________________
c) After the cinema I will go to McDonald's. You ______________________
d) Maybe we'll watch TV. Our neighbours ______________________

2 Frage nach dem unterstrichenen Satzteil.

a) It will rain tomorrow. When ______________________?
b) I will sell my old computer. ______________________?
c) Our aunt will visit us next month. ______________________?
d) Bill will sing a song on my birthday.
______________________?

In älteren englischen Texten findet man in der ersten Person Singular und Plural noch das Wort "shall" an der Stelle von "will". Heute wird "shall" meist nur noch verwendet, wenn man einen Vorschlag macht.

Shall I sing a song for you? Shall we go now?

Vergleich der Futurformen

Neben dem going-to-Futur und dem will-Futur gibt es noch eine weitere Möglichkeit, über zukünftige Ereignisse zu sprechen. Wenn man im Englischen über Ereignisse redet, die in der Zukunft liegen und schon beschlossene Sache sind, verwendet man häufig einfach die Verlaufsform der Gegenwart, besonders dann, wenn es sich um Ereignisse handelt, denen man mit Freude oder innerer Spannung entgegensieht.

What are you doing this evening?
This evening I'm playing tennis with my girlfriend.

Bei den folgenden adverbialen Bestimmungen der Zeit wird besonders häufig die Verlaufsform der Gegenwart verwendet, um zukünftige Ereignisse zu beschreiben.

tomorrow	this evening	next Monday / Tuesday / Wednesday …
soon	tonight	this afternoon

1 Die folgenden Sätze sollen zukünftige Ereignisse beschreiben. Verwende dazu die Verlaufsform der Gegenwart wie im Beispiel.

a) We / to leave / this afternoon
We are leaving this afternoon.

b) for New York / the boat / to leave / on Monday

______

c) tomorrow / we / to listen / to the radio

______

d) this afternoon / my parents / to fly / to London

______

2 Trage die Sätze in die Tabelle ein.

We're going to the theatre next Friday.
I'm going to feed my dog.
My uncle is coming this afternoon.
The plane is going to take off in one minute.

Verlaufsform der Gegenwart	going-to-Futur
a) ______	a) ______
______	______
b) ______	b) ______
______	______

Ob man eine zukünftige Handlung besser mit “going to” oder mit der Verlaufsform der Gegenwart ausdrücken sollte, ist nicht immer leicht zu entscheiden. Manchmal sind beide Möglichkeiten richtig oder sie unterscheiden sich nur geringfügig.

Don’t worry, Mum. I’m going to do my homework in a few minutes.

Don’t worry, Mum. I’m doing my homework soon.

Wichtiger ist es, das Futur mit “going to” und das Futur mit “will” richtig unterscheiden zu können.

Futur mit “going to”

Dinge, die man in der Zukunft plant oder beabsichtigt

I’m going to swim.
She’s going to listen to music.
We’re going to eat hamburgers.

Futur mit “will”

a) Dinge, die in der Zukunft passieren werden, ohne dass man einen Einfluss darauf hat
b) Dinge, die vermutlich passieren werden

I’ll see my friends at school.
I think I’ll get lots of money for this guitar.
Maybe we’ll spend our holidays in Italy.

1 Entscheide, ob du in den folgenden Sätzen das Futur mit “going to” oder das Futur mit “will” gebrauchen musst. Das Verb, das du verwenden sollst, steht am Ende des Satzes in der Klammer.

a) We ______________________ the new film. (to watch)
b) Maybe it ______________________ tomorrow. (to be nice weather)
c) I think you ______________ the tennis match next Sunday. (to win)
d) My sister ______________________. (to make a cake)
e) I’m sure Grandpa ______________________ this afternoon. (to work)

2 Welcher Satz passt zu welchem Bild? Trage den Buchstaben ein.

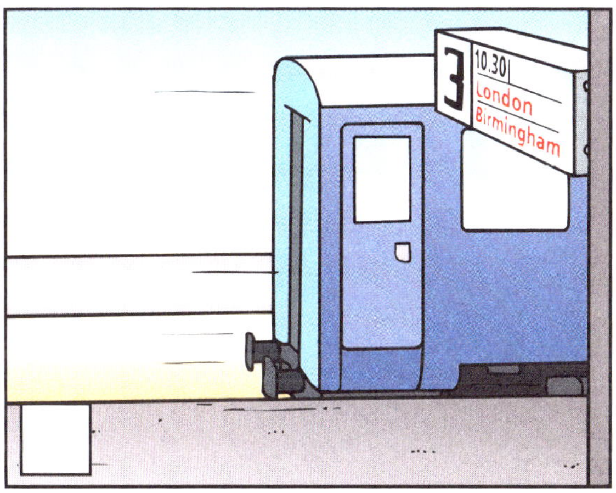

a) Tomorrow I'm going to visit my sister in Birmingham.
b) The train will leave on platform 3 at half past ten.

Die einfache Vergangenheit (simple past)

Im Englischen wird die einfache Vergangenheit (simple past) bei vielen Verben gebildet, indem an den Infinitiv des Verbs die Endung -ed angehängt wird.

to ask	–	I ask**ed**	to shout	–	we shout**ed**
to clean	–	you clean**ed**	to watch	–	you watch**ed**
to open	–	he open**ed**	to listen	–	they listen**ed**
to paint	–	she paint**ed**	to bark	–	it bark**ed**

Mit der einfachen Vergangenheitsform drückt man aus, dass ein Ereignis zu einem ganz bestimmten Zeitpunkt stattgefunden hat. Oft findet man in diesem Zusammenhang diese adverbialen Bestimmungen der Zeit:

last Monday … last week … last year … last month …
in 1848 … yesterday … 2nd May, 1952 … in January …

In 1492 Columbus discover**ed** America.
It rain**ed** last Wednesday.
We watch**ed** TV last night.
I call**ed** my friend yesterday.

1 Schreibe jeweils das Verb in der einfachen Vergangenheit auf.

a) to answer
I ______
Nick ______
You ______

b) to walk
You ______
She ______
The girls ______

c) to shout
Kate ______
We ______
You ______

d) to listen
He ______
We ______
They ______

e) to work
You ______
She ______
The men ______

f) to open
Ken ______
He ______
You ______

2 Die Bilder zeigen dir Dinge, die im letzten Urlaub passiert sind. Schreibe jeweils einen Satz in der einfachen Vergangenheit auf.

to climb up a tree

to walk into a cave

to play tennis

a) We ______
b) We ______
c) We ______

Besondere Schreibweisen bei regelmäßigen Verben

Wenn ein Infinitiv mit einem -e endet, wird in der einfachen Vergangenheit nur noch ein -d angehängt.

to arrive	–	you arrive**d**
to phone	–	he phone**d**
to live	–	they live**d**
to cycle	–	we cycle**d**

Wenn Verben nach einem einzelnen kurzen Vokal mit einem einzelnen Konsonanten enden (-p, -b, -t, -d, -g, -m, -n), dann wird dieser Konsonant verdoppelt.

to stop	–	we stop**ped**
to plan	–	you plan**ned**
to drop	–	it drop**ped**

Wenn ein -y als letzter Buchstabe auf einen Konsonanten folgt, wird es zu einem -i.

to try	–	I tr**ied**
to cry	–	you cr**ied**
to carry	–	we carr**ied**

1 Setze das Verb in der einfachen Vergangenheit ein. Achte auf die verschiedenen besonderen Schreibweisen.

a) We ______________________ at Cologne yesterday. (to arrive)
b) They ______________________ their relatives in France. (to visit)
c) He ______________________ from Wales to Scotland. (to move)
d) We ______________________ to spend our holidays in Ireland. (to plan)
e) She ______________________ at the traffic lights. (to stop)
f) He ______________________ to repair his bike. (to try)

2 Welcher Satz passt zu dem Bild? Trage den richtigen Buchstaben ein.

a) We watched TV yesterday.
b) Mum watched TV yesterday.
c) Mum is watching TV now.
d) Sally is watching TV now.

Wenn im Deutschen etwas vor einiger Zeit geschehen ist, wird das im Englischen mit dem Wort “ago” ausgedrückt.

I called you a week ago.
My father stopped smoking three years ago.

Die einfache Vergangenheit mit unregelmäßigen Verben

Bei einer ganzen Reihe häufig gebrauchter Verben wird die Vergangenheitsform nicht durch das Anhängen von -e an den Infinitiv gebildet. Sie haben eine eigenständige Vergangenheitsform, die in allen Personen gleich ist. Diese Verben heißen unregelmäßige Verben. Hier sind einige davon:

Infinitiv	Vergangenheit	Infinitiv	Vergangenheit
to buy	bought	to have	had
to do	did	to make	made
to eat	ate	to meet	met
to give	gave	to sell	sold
to go	went	to take	took

Eine Liste mit diesen und anderen unregelmäßigen Verben steht auf den Seiten 120 / 121. Du musst diese Verben unbedingt auswendig können!

1 Setze die richtige Vergangenheitsform des unregelmäßigen Verbs ein.

a) On Sunday Harry ________________ a bus to the stadium. (to take)
b) On the island they ________________ fish. (to sell)
c) I ________________ to the circus. (to go)
d) We ________________ a lot of popcorn. (to buy)
e) I ________________ my friend at the bus station. (to meet)
f) We ________________ our homework in the afternoon. (to do)
g) Kim and Jenny ________________ dinner in a restaurant. (to have)
h) Sidney ________________ some shrimps at the port. (to eat)
i) The monsters in the film ________________ a terrible noise. (to make)

In der Gegenwart wird „haben / besitzen“ im Englischen mit “have got” ausgedrückt. In der Vergangenheit sagt man aber im Englischen nur noch “had”. Das Hilfsverb “must” hat keine Vergangenheit. Es wird dann mit “to have to” umschrieben. Vergleiche dazu die folgenden Sätze.

Billy has got a tiny little cat.	Billy had a tiny little cat.
He must feed it every day.	He had to feed it every day.

Die Vergangenheitsform von "to be"

Im Gegensatz zu allen anderen unregelmäßigen Verben unterscheidet sich die Vergangenheitsform von "to be" auch abhängig von der jeweiligen Person.

I was sick last week.
You were …

He was hungry at night.
She was …
It was …

We were in Spain last year.
You were …
They were …

Das Verb "to be" verneint man in der Vergangenheitsform durch das Anhängen von "not". Dabei gibt es wieder eine Kurzform, die sowohl im gesprochenen als auch im geschriebenen Englisch verwendet wird.

I wasn't angry with him.
You weren't …

He wasn't too late.
She wasn't …
It wasn't …

We weren't the winner today.
You weren't …
They weren't …

Fragen werden mit "to be" durch die Umstellung von Subjekt und Prädikat gestellt. Auf Entscheidungsfragen antwortet man mit einer Kurzantwort, die das Verb wiederholt.

Were you happy to meet your friend? .... Yes, I was.
Was he at the cinema last week? .... No, he wasn't.
Where were Sally and Kate yesterday? .... They were at the zoo.
When were you in Dublin? .... I was in Dublin last year.

1 Setze in die folgenden Sätze richtig "were" oder "was" ein.

a) We ______ in London and visited the tower.
b) My friend Harry ______ ill last week.
c) Jill's parents ______ in England.
d) My friends and I ______ late for the film.

2 Fülle die Lücken wie im Beispiel aus.

a) Were you at school yesterday? Yes, I was.
b) ______ Henry at the cinema yesterday? No, ______.
c) ______ you in Denmark last summer? Yes, we ______.
d) ______ you on the sports field last week? No, I ______.

Im Englischen gibt es für das Hilfsverb "can" die Vergangenheitsform "could". Weil "could" aber auch „könnte" bedeutet, umschreibt man es sehr oft mit einer Form von "to be able to", wenn es „können" bedeuten soll.

"I was able to read when I was five."
"I don't believe that! You weren't able to count to ten!"

Die Verneinung in der einfachen Vergangenheit

Nur Hilfsverben wie “to be” können durch die Ergänzung mit “not” verneint werden. In der einfachen Vergangenheit setzt man deshalb das Hilfsverb “to do” vor den Infinitiv des Verbs, um verneinte Aussagesätze zu formulieren. Die Form “did not” bleibt in allen Personen gleich. Fast immer wird die Kurzform “didn’t” gesprochen und geschrieben.

I **didn’t** play in the garden.
You **didn’t** walk down the street.
He **didn’t** write a letter.
She **didn’t** watch the bank robbery.
It **didn’t** run away.

We **didn’t** play tennis.
You **didn’t** clean your shoes.
They **didn’t** help their parents.

Hierbei muss unbedingt beachtet werden, dass das Vollverb im **Infinitiv** steht. Auf keinen Fall darf hier die Vergangenheitsform verwendet oder ein -s in der 3. Person Singular ergänzt werden!

He **didn’t watch** TV.

She **didn’t visit** her grandparents.

1 Beim Besuch auf dem Bauernhof wollten die Kinder nicht mithelfen. Schreibe verneinte Aussagesätze wie im Beispiel. Achte besonders darauf, dass das Vollverb im Infinitiv steht.

a) Mr Miller milked the cows. Sandra didn’t milk the cows.
b) Mrs Miller collected eggs. Kevin ______________________
c) The farmer made hay. The children ______________________
d) Grandpa watered the vegetables. Greg ______________________
e) Grandma fed the pigs. The girls ______________________
f) The Millers picked apples. The boys ______________________
g) Mr Miller repaired the tractor. Tom ______________________

Wenn “to do” in einer fester Verbindung auftaucht, dann ist es ein Vollverb und wird ebenfalls mit “didn’t” verneint. Dasselbe gilt für “to have” in der Bedeutung „besitzen“ oder in anderen festen Verbindungen.

We didn’t do the shopping.
I didn’t have a shower.

She didn’t have any pets.

Fragen in der einfachen Vergangenheit

Auch bei der Formulierung von Fragen verwendet man das Hilfsverb "to do". In der einfachen Vergangenheit wird also mit "did" gefragt. Bei Entscheidungsfragen folgt darauf eine Kurzantwort.

Did you help your uncle yesterday? .... Yes, I did.

Selbstverständlich steht dabei das Verb im Infinitiv und nicht in der Vergangenheitsform oder mit einem -s in der 3. Person Singular.

Did you enjoy your holiday in Sweden? Did he clean the car?

Fragen mit "when" stehen immer in der einfachen Vergangenheit. Wenn auf Fragen mit Fragewörtern in einem vollständigen Satz geantwortet wird, dann steht in der Antwort natürlich wieder die einfache Form der Vergangenheit.

When did we move from Berlin to Hamburg? .... We moved in 1998.
When did you watch TV? .... I watched TV last night.
Where did you go yesterday? .... Yesterday I went to the railway station.
What did the girls do last Saturday? .... They swam in the river last Saturday.
Who did you meet yesterday? .... I met Emma yesterday.

1 Schreibe jeweils die Kurzantwort auf die Frage auf.

a) Did Willy have much money? No, ______________________.
b) Did you see the moon last night? Yes, we ______________________.
c) Did you drive fast with your new car? Yes, I ______________________.
d) Did she feed her pets every day? No, ______________________.

2 Hier werden Fragen mit einem ganzen Satz beantwortet. Setze die richtige Verbform ein. Schau dazu bei der Liste der unregelmäßigen Verben auf Seite 120 / 121 nach.

a) Did you sleep in your bed? No, I ______________________ in my tent.
b) Did you win the race with your friend? Yes, I ______________ the race.
c) Did you sit in the kitchen? No, we ______________ in the living room.
d) Did you hear the birds singing? Yes, I ______________ the birds singing.
e) Did you catch a fish? No, I ______________ an old shoe.
f) Did you go home after the party?
Yes, I ______________ home.

Wenn das Fragewort "who" die deutsche Bedeutung „wer" hat, umschreibt man nicht mit "to do".

Who told you to go to bed? Who helped you when you were sick?

Die Verlaufsform der Vergangenheit (past progressive)

So wie in der Gegenwart gibt es auch in der Vergangenheit eine Verlaufsform. Sie wird mit "was" bzw. "were" und der -ing-Form des Verbs gebildet.

I **was** walk**ing**
you **were** learn**ing**

he **was** play**ing**
she **was** sing**ing**
it **was** crawl**ing**

we **were** work**ing**
you **were** eat**ing**
they **were** read**ing**

Mit der Verlaufsform der Vergangenheit (past progressive) beschreibt man Dinge, die zu einem ganz bestimmten Zeitpunkt in der Vergangenheit gerade geschahen. Hierauf weisen genaue Zeitbezeichnungen hin, wie:

at three o'clock	Yesterday at three o'clock the sun was shining.
a quarter to nine	But it was raining at a quarter to nine.
at midnight	Our visitors were leaving us at midnight.

Der genaue Zeitpunkt kann auch dadurch beschrieben werden, dass in einem Nebensatz ein anderes Ereignis gleichzeitig stattfand, begann oder endete.

I was writing a letter when my uncle came in.
The people were crowding around when the alarm rang.
When you called I was just doing my homework.

1 Schreibe das Verb in der Verlaufsform der Vergangenheit auf.

a) (to dream) I was dreaming ______
b) (to run) You ______
c) (to come) Cedric ______
d) (to shout) We ______
e) (to listen) They ______
f) (to go) She ______

2 Nur ein Satz passt zum Bild. Kreuze ihn an.

a) Nelly was watching TV when the telephone rang.
b) The telephone was ringing when Nelly wasn't at home.
c) Nelly was writing an e-mail when the telephone rang.
d) The telephone was ringing when Nelly came in.

Wie die -ing-Form des Verbs in besonderen Fällen gebildet wird, wurde auf Seite 72 genauer beschrieben.

to make – making
to stop – stopping

Verneinte Sätze mit der Verlaufsform der Vergangenheit bildet man mit “was not” und “were not” bzw. den Kurzformen “wasn’t” und “weren’t”.

I wasn’t reading at three o’clock. You weren’t sleeping at midnight.

Bei Fragen vertauschen Subjekt und Prädikat (also “was” bzw. “were”) ihre Stellung.

What were you doing at eight o’clock yesterday?

Auf Entscheidungsfragen folgt eine Kurzantwort, in der “was” bzw. “were” wiederholt wird.

Were you playing computer games?.............Yes, I was.
Were you dancing?..Yes, we were.
Was he walking in the garden? ....No, he wasn’t.
Were they listening to the radio?....................No, they weren’t.

1 Was taten die Familienmitglieder gestern Abend um 9 Uhr? Bilde jeweils verneinte Sätze.

a) Mum was watching TV. Dad wasn’t watching TV.
b) Dad was playing computer games. Sarah ____________________.
c) Sarah was reading a book. Keith ____________________.
d) Keith was painting a picture. The twins ____________________.
e) The twins were sleeping. Grandpa ____________________.
f) Grandpa was smoking a pipe. Grandma ____________________.
g) Grandma was eating chocolate. The dogs ____________________.

2 Schreibe die Kurzantwort auf.

a) Were the birds singing? Yes, ____________________.
b) Were you drinking coffee? No, we ____________________.
c) Was he driving a car? No, ____________________.
d) Were you riding a horse? Yes, I ____________________.

Das Perfekt (present perfect)

Um Ereignisse oder Handlungen zu beschreiben, die zu einem unbestimmten Zeitpunkt in der Vergangenheit stattgefunden haben, verwendet man im Englischen das Perfekt (present perfect). Es setzt sich aus "have" bzw. "has" und dem Partizip Perfekt zusammen. Das Partizip Perfekt wird bei regelmäßigen Verben genauso wie die Vergangenheitsform gebildet, indem an den Infinitiv -ed angehängt wird.

I'**ve** listen**ed** to the radio.
You'**ve** clos**ed** the windows.
He **has** stopp**ed** talking.
She **has** open**ed** the door.
It **has** rain**ed** until now.
We'**ve** work**ed** hard.
You'**ve** play**ed** badminton.
They'**ve** learn**ed** their lesson.

Signalwörter wie "just" oder "already" weisen darauf hin, dass ein Ereignis in der Vergangenheit Auswirkungen in der Gegenwart hat. Auch dann wird das Perfekt verwendet. "Just" und "already" stehen zwischen "have / has" und dem Partizip.

He has already arrived.
I've just lost my umbrella.

1 Bilde jeweils die Perfektform mit dem angegebenen Verb.

a) I ______________ (to wash)
b) You ______________ (to clean)
c) He ______________ (to visit)
d) We ______________ (to walk)
e) They ______________ (to paint)
f) You ______________ (to try)
g) It ______________ (to rest)
h) She ______________ (to laugh)

2 Welcher Satz wird auf welchem Bild gesagt?
Schreibe den Buchstaben in das Kästchen.

a) "We are washing our car."
b) "We've just washed our car."
c) "We washed our car yesterday."

Anders als im Deutschen stehen im Englischen Objekt oder adverbiale Bestimmung immer erst nach dem Partizip.

He has already cleaned his shoes. We have just arrived at the holiday camp.

Das Perfekt mit unregelmäßigen Verben

Eine Reihe häufig gebrauchter Verben hat ein eigenes Partizip, das meist nicht mit der Vergangenheitsform übereinstimmt. In den Listen mit unregelmäßigen Verben findet man das Partizip immer nach dem Infinitiv und der Vergangenheit an dritter Stelle, so wie bei diesen Verben. Vergleiche dazu auch die Liste mit diesen und anderen unregelmäßigen Verben auf den Seiten 120 / 121. Du musst diese Verben unbedingt auswendig können!

Infinitiv	Vergangenheit	Perfekt
to be	was	been
to break	broke	broken
to come	came	come
to eat	ate	eaten
to have	had	had
to pay	paid	paid
to put	put	put
to run	ran	run
to steal	stole	stolen
to take	took	taken
to write	wrote	written

1 Jemand hat einen Überfall beobachtet und berichtet aufgeregt, was er gerade erlebt hat. Setze die richtigen Perfektformen ein. Achtung: Zwei Verben sind unregelmäßig!

a) I ________ just ________ a bank robbery. (to watch)
b) The thieves ____________________ away. (to run)
c) They ________________________ a lot of money. (to steal)
d) They ____________________ a lot of people. (to frighten)

2 Regelmäßiges oder unregelmäßiges Verb? Verwende das Perfekt und setze jeweils das richtige Partizip ein.

a) He ______________ (to listen)
b) We ______________ (to break)
c) They ______________ (to work)
d) You ______________ (to pay)
e) She ______________ (to go)
f) I ______________ (take)
g) You ______________ (to write)
h) We ______________ (to eat)

Im Deutschen werden die Verben der Bewegung im Perfekt mit „sein“ gebildet, im Englischen immer mit “have” bzw. “has”.

Ich bin gerade weggerannt.	I've just run away.
Ich bin gerade über einen Zaun gesprungen.	I've just jumped over a fence.

Verneinung und Fragen im Perfekt

Bei der Bildung des Perfekts ist “to have” ein Hilfsverb. Deshalb werden verneinte Sätze im Perfekt durch das Anhängen von “not” gebildet, fast immer mit den Kurzformen “haven’t” bzw. “hasn’t”.

I haven’t brushed my teeth.
You haven’t brushed your teeth.
He hasn’t brushed his teeth.
She hasn’t brushed her teeth.
It hasn’t brushed its teeth.

We haven’t brushed our teeth.
You haven’t brushed your teeth.
They haven’t brushed their teeth.

Grundsätzlich wird bei Fragen das Perfekt verwendet, wenn man danach fragt, ob etwas geschehen ist. Bei Fragen im Perfekt tauschen Subjekt und Hilfsverb ihre Stellung. Auf Entscheidungsfragen folgt eine Kurzantwort, bei der das Hilfsverb wiederholt wird.

Have you done your homework yet? Yes, I have.
Has Sally ridden a horse yet? No, she hasn’t.
Has Ben broken his arm? Yes, he has.
Have you washed your hair yet? No, we haven’t.

“Yet” steht immer am Ende des Satzes. Es bedeutet „schon“.
In verneinten Sätzen bedeutet es aber „noch nicht“.

Have you seen Dad yet? No, I haven’t seen him yet.

1 Die Kinder haben ihre Aufgaben noch nicht erledigt. Schreibe verneinte Sätze im Perfekt und beende sie mit “yet”.

a) Robby hasn’t washed his hair yet. (to wash his hair)
b) Daniel ______________________ (to do his homework)
c) Dave ______________________ (to feed his rabbit)
d) Mary ______________________ (to clean her room)
e) Jane ______________________ (to do the shopping)

2 Beantworte die Fragen mit der passenden Kurzantwort.

a) Have you ever been to London? No, we ______________.
b) Has Mr Smith bought a new car yet? Yes, ______________.
c) Have you stolen the lady’s handbag? No, I ______________.
d) Have you had dinner yet? Yes, we ______________.
e) Has Mum already done the shopping? Yes, ______________.

Vergleich von einfacher Vergangenheit und Perfekt

Weil sich der englische Sprachgebrauch vom deutschen unterscheidet, ist es wichtig darauf zu achten, wann im Englischen die einfache Vergangenheit benutzt wird und wann das Perfekt. Vergleiche dazu die folgenden Sätze.

Einfache Vergangenheit:

a) Etwas ist zu einem ganz bestimmten Zeitpunkt geschehen (yesterday, two hours ago, on Saturday, in 2002 ...)

I lost my umbrella a week ago.
I suppose Carol brushed her teeth four weeks ago.
We didn't meet him yesterday.

b) Bei Fragen, wann etwas geschehen ist

When did you see your friend?
When did we go to Birmingham?

Perfekt:

a) Etwas ist zu einem unbestimmten Zeitpunkt in der Vergangenheit oder eben gerade geschehen (just, already, yet)

Oh, what's that? I've lost my umbrella.
Don't worry, Mum. I've just brushed my teeth!
I haven't met him yet.

b) Bei Fragen, ob etwas geschehen ist

Have you seen your friend?
Have you been to Birmingham?

1 Überlege, ob der jeweilige Satz in der einfachen Vergangenheit oder im Perfekt steht. Setze dann die richtige Form ein.

a) I ____________________ my grandparents last year. (to visit)
b) We ____________________ just now. (to have breakfast)
c) My father ____________________ an accident last summer. (to have)
d) He ____________________ into the library last week. (to go)
e) She ____________________ her pencil an hour ago. (to find)

2 Welcher Satz passt zum Bild? Schreibe den Buchstaben in das Kästchen.

a) He has just found his glasses.
b) He found his glasses yesterday.
c) I haven't eaten an apple yet.
d) I ate some apples yesterday.
e) The train has just left the station.
f) The train left half an hour ago.

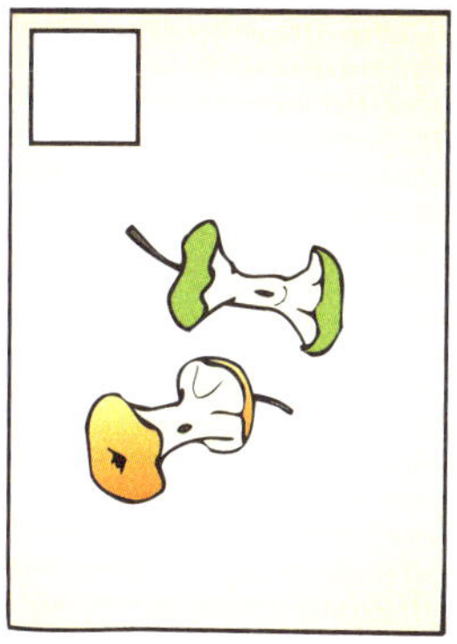

Funktion und Bildung des Gerundiums

Um im Englischen Tätigkeiten als Nomen zu gebrauchen, wird die -ing-Form des Verbs verwendet. Sie wird dann Gerundium (gerund) genannt.

Boxing is my favourite sport.

Fishing is my hobby.

Für die Bildung des Gerundiums gelten dieselben Regeln wie für die -ing-Form bei der Verlaufsform. Also:

regelmäßig	**-e am Ende entfällt**	**doppelter Konsonant nach kurzem Vokal**	**aus -ie wird -y**
to walk – walking	to drive – driving	to run – running	to lie – lying
to be – being	to have – having	to put – putting	to die – dying
to go – going	to come – coming	to stop – stopping	

Das Gerundium darf jedoch nicht mit der Verlaufsform verwechselt werden!

Gerundium

Eating in a restaurant is fun.
Feeding the cats is your job.

Verlaufsform

We are **eating** in a restaurant.
Vic is **feeding** the cats now.

1 Schreibe die entsprechenden Tätigkeiten unter die Bilder. Verwende das Gerundium.

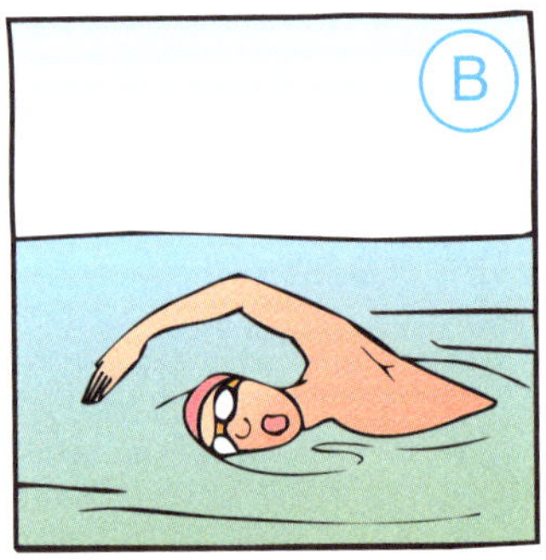

to fish
to run
to ski
to swim
to jump
to box

2 Welcher Satz enthält ein Gerundium? Kreuze an.

a) Climbing is dangerous.
b) Reading books is very interesting.
c) Our cat is climbing up the tree.
d) The children are watching TV.
e) Pat is reading a book now.
f) Watching TV is sometimes great.

Das Gerundium als Subjekt

Wenn man ähnlich gebaute Sätze vergleicht, wird besonders deutlich, dass das Gerundium im Englischen an die Stelle eines Nomens tritt.

Stop the train.
Stop talking.

Swimming is fun.
Hockey is fun.

Dementsprechend steht ein Verb nach einem Gerundium als Subjekt auch in der 3. Person Singular.

Smoking endangers your health.

Beim Übersetzen ins Deutsche wird ein Gerundium aber nicht immer als Nomen wiedergegeben, sondern oft auch durch einen Infinitiv.

Going to the youth club is fun. – Es macht Spaß, zum Jugendklub zu gehen.
Driving a car can be dangerous. – Es kann gefährlich sein, ein Auto zu fahren.

1 Welches Gerundium passt zu welchem Bild? Schreibe es darunter.

Dancing club | No smoking! | No fishing!

______ ______ ______

2 Übersetze diese Sätze ins Deutsche. Beachte, dass das Gerundium sowohl als Substantiv als auch als Infinitivkonstruktion übersetzt werden kann.

a) Swimming is fun.

______

b) Waiting for the bus makes me angry.

______

c) Singing is Sally's hobby.

______

d) Coming home is always great.

______

Das Gerundium als Objekt

Es gibt eine Anzahl von Verben, nach denen ein weiteres Verb als Gerundium folgt und somit die Stelle eines Objekts einnimmt:

I enjoy playing the guitar.

Dad suggested eating in a restaurant.

Hier sind die häufigsten Verben, auf die ein Gerundium folgen muss:

to admit	to avoid	to enjoy	to give up	to go on
to imagine	to miss	to practise	to risk	to suggest

Nach einigen anderen häufig verwendeten Verben kann sowohl ein Gerundium als auch ein Infinitiv verwendet werden. Der Sinn der entsprechenden Sätze ist völlig gleich.

to begin   to start   to love   to hate   to like

I like to ride a horse.
I like riding a horse.

You hate to do your homework.
You hate doing your homework.

1 Die Familie ist aus dem Urlaub zurück. Für jeden war etwas anderes wichtig. Schau auf das Bild und ergänze die Sätze.

getting wet   playing computer games   getting sunburn   playing with other children

a) Dad avoided ______________________

b) Willy missed ______________________

c) Mary liked ______________________

d) Mum risked ______________________

2 Bei welchem der Sätze aus Übung 1 könnte auch der Infinitiv statt des Gerundiums verwendet werden? Satz ________

3 Welchen Satz könnte der Vater auf dem Bild sagen? Kreuze ihn an.

a) Stop walking now.
b) Let's go on walking.
c) You enjoy walking very much.
d) Please avoid walking too much.

Das Gerundium nach Präpositionen

Wenn auf eine Präposition ein Verb folgt, wird immer das Gerundium verwendet. Hier sind einige Adjektive mit Präpositionen, nach denen ein Gerundium stehen muss:

afraid **of**	good **at**	crazy **about**	Mum is good at cooking.
tired **of**	bad **at**	famous **for**	I'm tired of waiting.
proud **of**	angry **at**	interested **in**	Dad is interested in repairing cars.

Auf die folgenden Verben, die mit einer Präposition verbunden sind, muss ebenfalls das Gerundium folgen:

to dream **of**	to think **of**	to talk **about**	Many boys dream of being older.
to believe **in**	to look forward **to**		What do you think about going home?

1 Sieh dir die Bilder gut an. Setze den passenden Satzteil ein.

proud of having many friends
interested in repairing old clocks
crazy about playing computer games
dreaming of being a piano player
crazy about meeting her boyfriend
looking forward to having a party

a) Dennis is ____________________

b) Dad is ____________________

c) Patty is ____________________

d) Tanja is ____________________

e) Bob is ____________________

f) Pia is ____________________

Die Fragewörter "who" und "what"

Mit dem Fragewort "who" fragt man nach Personen, mit "what" fragt man nach Dingen. Manchmal sind "who" oder "what" das Subjekt eines Satzes. Dann benötigt man zur Fragestellung kein Hilfsverb.

Who sells bikes?
Mr Keiton sells bikes.

What makes you happy?
Going on holiday makes me happy.

Wenn aber ein anderes Subjekt in der Frage vorhanden ist, wird mit "who" und "what" nach einem Objekt gefragt. Falls kein Hilfsverb vorhanden ist, benötigt man eine Umschreibung mit "to do".

Fragen mit Hilfsverb

What are you going to buy?
What is the teacher talking about?
Who will Bill meet next Friday?
Who are you helping with his homework?

Fragen ohne Hilfsverb

What did you buy yesterday?
What does the teacher usually talk about?
Who did Bill meet at work?
Who does Mum help with the cooking?

1 Überlege, welches Wort das Subjekt des Fragesatzes ist. Kreise es ein.

a) Who made that terrible noise?
b) What makes you angry?
c) Who am I going to help?
d) What are the children laughing at?
e) Who did Dad meet yesterday?
f) What is Sally going to do?
g) Who collects old clocks?
h) What cries in the garden at night?

2 Lies die Fragen und kreuze die richtigen Antworten an.

a) Who has got a yellow shirt? o David o Kevin o Marvin
b) Who does Marvin see? o David o Kevin
c) Who is sitting in the tree? o Kevin o Marvin o David
d) What makes a terrible noise? o the horse o the dog
e) What is Marvin's dog doing? o sleeping o barking
f) Who likes to eat ice cream? o David o Kevin o Marvin

Die Fragewörter "whose" und "which"

Mit "whose" wird danach gefragt, wem etwas gehört. In der Antwort auf eine solche Frage wird immer entweder der s-Genitiv oder ein Possessivpronomen verwendet (mine, yours, his, hers, its, ours, yours, theirs).

"Whose dog is barking?" ...."Kitty's." .... "Hers."
"Whose books are these?" ...."The teachers'." .... "Theirs."
"Whose basket is this?" ...."Bello's." .... "His."

Das Fragewort "which" verwendet man, wenn man etwas über Dinge und Personen erfahren will, die zu einer begrenzten Anzahl gehören.

unbegrenzte Anzahl – "who" oder "what"	**begrenzte Anzahl – "which"**
Who sings the loudest?	Which of your friends sings the loudest?
What colours are Ann's shirt?	Which colour do you prefer?

1 Schau dir das Bild an und beantworte die Fragen – zuerst mit dem Nomen, dann mit dem Possessivpronomen, wie im Beispiel.

		Nomen	Possessivpronomen
a)	Whose shoes are black?	Susan's.	Hers.
b)	Whose trousers are green?	______	______
c)	Whose basket is blue?	______	______
d)	Whose sweatshirt is red?	______	______
e)	Whose skin is black and white?	______	______
f)	Whose shirt is white?	______	______

2 Überlege, ob du hier "what" bzw. "who" oder "which" einsetzen musst.

a) ______________ would you like to eat?
b) ______________ of you liked the party?
c) ______________ colour is your car?
d) ______________ visited the zoo yesterday?
e) ______________ boy from your form do you like most?
f) ______________ of these books are Sally's?
g) ______________ drink do you prefer – tea or lemon juice?

Question tags

Eine Besonderheit im gesprochenen Englischen ist die Angewohnheit, an einen Aussagesatz eine kurze Frage anzuhängen. Solche Ergänzungen werden "question tags" genannt. Sie bedeuten so viel wie „oder?“ bzw. „nicht wahr?“.

It's a nice day, isn't it? You don't like fish, do you? That's right, isn't it?

Question tags werden mit einem Hilfsverb und dem Personalpronomen gebildet.

Bei bejahten Aussagesätzen stehen die question tags in der verneinten Form.

Mike will go to London, won't he?
We are quite happy, aren't we?
Ken has got a new computer, hasn't he?

Bei verneinten Aussagesätzen stehen die question tags dagegen in der bejahten Form.

We don't like horror videos, do we?
Mr Smith didn't talk much, did he?
Pam can't drive a car, can she?

1 Ergänze die Sätze mit den dazugehörigen question tags.

hasn't he? has he? can't you? is she? isn't she? can you?

a) Mr Smith has got a little daughter, ______
b) You can hear the bird sing, ______
c) Mary is a lucky girl, ______
d) Barry hasn't done his homework yet, ______
e) Mrs Baker isn't a good piano player, ______
f) You can't understand Russian, ______

2 Setze passende question tags ein.

a) The teachers are early today, ______
b) Pete can't understand geography, ______
c) Kate is old enough to go to the disco, ______
d) This winter has been very cold, ______
e) Your little sister isn't sleeping, ______
f) Children don't like to brush their teeth, ______
g) We can't rent this house, ______

Wenn im Aussagesatz kein anderes Hilfsverb verwendet wird, dann benutzt man bei den question tags die entsprechende Form von "to do". Dabei muss man darauf achten, ob der Satz in der Gegenwarts- oder in der Vergangenheitsform steht.

Gegenwart

We usually swim on Saturdays, don't we?
Harry often plays computer games, doesn't he?

Vergangenheit

Your parents came home very late last night, didn't they?
Robin's father worked at BBC London, didn't he?

1 Verwende bei den question tags die richtige Form von "to do".
Achte auf die Zeit, in der der Aussagesatz steht.

a) Charles doesn't speak German, ____________________
b) Our team lost the football game, ____________________
c) Girls usually like horses, ____________________
d) Ben loves Anna, ____________________
e) Your girlfriend collected stamps, ____________________
f) It often rains in Great Britain, ____________________

2 Enthält der Satz ein Hilfsverb oder musst du mit einer Form von "to do" umschreiben?
Ergänze die richtigen question tags.

a) Eliza won't go to London, ____________________
b) We saw a great rainbow yesterday, ____________________
c) Look outside, it is raining, ____________________
d) Lions eat meat, ____________________
e) I usually play tennis on Sundays, ____________________
f) Crocodiles are dangerous, ____________________

Beachte die folgenden beiden besonderen Formen von question tags.

I'm a very lucky person, **aren't I**?
There weren't many wild animals in the zoo, **were there**?

Konjunktionen

Mit Konjunktionen (Bindewörtern) verbindet man Wörter und Wortgruppen.

Do you want tea **or** coffee? We've got many horses **and** some cows.

Wenn Haupt- und Nebensätze mit einer Konjunktion verbunden werden, dann bringt sie zum Ausdruck, in welchem logischen Zusammenhang die Sätze miteinander stehen. Im Gegensatz zum Deutschen steht dabei zwischen Haupt- und Nebensatz kein Komma.

Jill and Fred can't visit you **because** they have no time.
Bill has got a new piano **but** he can't play.

Hier sind die häufigsten Konjunktionen, mit denen Haupt- und Nebensätze verbunden werden, und ihre deutschen Bedeutungen:

but – aber	before – bevor	because – weil
after – nachdem	that – dass	until – bis

1 Unterstreiche in diesen Sätzen jeweils die Konjunktion, die Haupt- und Nebensatz verbindet.

a) John didn't buy the book because it was too old.
b) Ann can read English newspapers but I can't.
c) I hope that you'll come in time.
d) Feed the cat before you play tennis.
e) I was still hungry after I ate the cake.
f) Harry waited in the rain until his girlfriend came.

2 Welcher der Sätze aus der ersten Aufgabe passt jeweils zum Bild? Schreibe den entsprechenden Buchstaben in den jeweiligen Kreis.

Einige englische Konjunktionen können leicht mit ähnlich lautenden deutschen Begriffen verwechselt werden. Man sollte sich ihre Bedeutung deshalb sehr gut einprägen.

englische Konjunktion	deutsche Bedeutung	Beispielsätze
so	deshalb, daher, also	It was too far **so** we took a taxi. I'm very sad **so** I can't laugh at your jokes.
while	während, währenddessen	Kim usually does her homework **while** she is watching TV. I sang **while** my brother played the guitar.
as	als, während	Mum has got sunburn **as** she lay on the beach. I cut my finger **as** I tried to repair my bike.
when	wenn (Gegenwart) als (Vergangenheit)	I usually sleep a little bit **when** I come from school. Grandpa slept the whole day **when** he was sick.

1 Ergänze die Hauptsätze mit dem passenden Nebensatz.

while you are listening to the radio
as it took off from the airport
when he was a little boy
so we had lots of fun in the swimming pool

a) Dave spent a lot of time in hospital ______________________
b) The weather was really nice ______________________
c) You can't learn English words ______________________
d) The plane made a terrible noise ______________________

2 Setze die passenden Konjunktionen ein.

but until because so when that

a) Hilary couldn't listen to her new record ________ the player was broken.
b) John wants to go on a journey ________ he has got no money.
c) The girls and boys entered the disco ________ the music began.
d) Do you know ________ my brother will marry his girlfriend next year?
e) It was too hot ________ I didn't work in the garden.
f) Ann must stay in hospital ________ she is in good health again.

Bedingungssätze mit "if"

In einem Bedingungssatz wird ausgedrückt, was geschehen wird, wenn eine bestimmte Bedingung erfüllt worden ist. Die Bedingung wird in einem Nebensatz genannt, der mit der Konjunktion "if" beginnt.

I will go swimming **if** the weather is fine.
We'll be too early **if** we start at nine o'clock.

Wenn der if-Satz am Anfang steht, werden beide Satzteile mit einem Komma getrennt, sonst aber nicht.

If the weather is bad, I will watch TV. If we start at ten o'clock, we'll be in time.

1 Ergänze die Satzanfänge mit dem entsprechenden Haupt- oder Nebensatz.

if you don't stop this music · she'll be very happy · if Mum gives us some money · he'll see his old friends · I'll buy a new bike · if they get a babysitter

a) If Emma meets Tim today ______
b) We'll go to the cinema ______
c) If I win a hundred pounds ______
d) Dad will get mad ______
e) If Bill comes to the disco ______
f) The Taylors will go to the theatre ______

2 Bei drei Sätzen aus der ersten Aufgabe musst du ein Komma zwischen Haupt- und Nebensatz setzen.
Welche Sätze sind das? ______ ______ ______

3 Welcher der Sätze aus der ersten Aufgabe passt jeweils zum Bild? Schreibe die entsprechenden Buchstaben in die Kreise.

Die Konjunktion "if" kann man im Deutschen mit „falls" übersetzen, aber auch mit „wenn". Man darf das englische Wort "if" deshalb auf keinen Fall mit dem englischen "when" durcheinanderbringen.

"when" – als, wenn ...

When Bill met Mary he invited her to dinner.
When Mrs Bean works in the garden she often finds snails in the salad.

"if" – falls (wenn)

Bill says: "If I meet Ben, I'll invite him, too."

Mrs Bean says: "If I find snails in the salad today, I'll kill them."

Der Hauptsatz steht fast immer im will-Futur, oder es wird ein Hilfsverb wie "can", "must" oder "should" gebraucht, dem ein Infinitiv folgt.
Der if-Satz steht grundsätzlich in der einfachen Gegenwart und niemals im will-Futur.

If you park here, I'll call the police!

If the coffee is too hot, you must wait a bit.

You'll be my best friend if you help me now.
We can go fishing if my uncle comes tomorrow.

1 "When" oder "if"? Setze die richtige Konjunktion ein.

a) ___________ father writes letters he hates noise.

b) We will visit Jim ___________ he invites us.

c) ___________ the sun shines, we can have a picnic in the wood.

d) The dog usually barks ___________ there is a strange person in the garden.

2 Setze die Verben in der richtigen Zeitform ein.

a) If we ___________ early (to be), we ___________ a good place in the cinema. (to get)

b) The children ___________ many friends (to invite) if the parents ___________ not at home. (to be)

c) If Dad ___________ home before 5 o'clock (to come), he ___________ to repair my bike. (to try)

d) Mr Smith ___________ us (to help) if we ___________ his shopping this week. (to do)

Manchmal werden mit if-Sätzen Aussagen gemacht, die allgemeingültig sind. Das "if" könnte man dann mit „immer dann, wenn..." übersetzen. In diesem Fall steht im Hauptsatz kein will-Futur, sondern die einfache Gegenwart.

If a hen grows old, it doesn't lay eggs any longer.

Die Relativpronomen "who", "which" und "that"

Wenn ein Nomen näher bestimmt werden soll, verwendet man dazu einen Relativsatz. Ohne diesen Relativsatz würde unklar bleiben, wer oder was gemeint ist. Relativsätze werden mit Relativpronomen eingeleitet. Bei Personen heißt das Relativpronomen "who".

Mrs Smith is the teacher **who** was in Scotland last year.
Mr Clueman is the neighbour **who** often repairs our bikes.

Wenn man über Sachen oder Tiere spricht, heißt das Relativpronomen "which".

The cows **which** are black and white belong to farmer Murphy.
The picture **which** hangs on the wall is from the 19th century.

Statt "who" und "which" kann man auch das Relativpronomen "that" verwenden. Bei Sachen und Tieren wird es häufig verwendet, bei Personen aber recht selten.

The cat **that** lies in the basket is mine.
I read a book about monsters **that** live in old castles.
The man **that** writes poems is going to visit us.

1 Setze das richtige Relativpronomen ein. Weil "that" immer möglich ist, sollst du dich bei dieser Aufgabe zwischen "who" und "which" entscheiden.

a) This is the train ____________ goes from London to Edinburgh.
b) There is the girl ____________ wrote some letters to me.
c) Show me the photos ____________ are in your bag.
d) Was it your sister ____________ won the tennis match?
e) Where is the postcard ____________ lay on the table?
f) The man ____________ works at BBC is my neighbour.

2 Trage die richtigen Namen in die Sätze ein.

Ella

Banjee

Marion

Hugh

Tibs

Phil

a) ____________ is the boy who has got a skateboard.
b) ____________ is the girl who is doing her homework.
c) ____________ is the cat which is sleeping on the floor.
d) ____________ is the boy who likes computer games.
e) ____________ is the girl who is going to have piano lessons.
f) ____________ is the cat which is walking on the shelf.

Die Relativpronomen als Subjekt und Objekt

Die Relativpronomen "who", "which" und "that" können das Subjekt des Relativsatzes sein.

The girl who is sitting next to me is my sister.
The bird that is swimming in the pond is a swan.

Relativpronomen können aber auch Objekt des Relativsatzes sein.

The girl who Mum met yesterday had a red shirt.
The bird that I have seen in the pond is a swan.

1 Überlege, ob das Relativpronomen Subjekt oder Objekt des Relativsatzes ist. Trage die Sätze richtig in die Tabelle ein.

a) The bike which I bought last week is already broken.
b) The doctor who visited me is a good one.
c) The chair which was broken is now ok.
d) The dress which Sally is wearing is nice.

Subjektstellung	Objektstellung

2 Verbinde die beiden Sätze jeweils mit einem Relativpronomen, so wie im Beispiel. Weil das Relativpronomen "that" immer möglich ist, entscheide dich zwischen "who" und "which".

a) The teacher will move to London next year. He is a good football player.
The teacher who is a good football player will move to London next year.

b) The plane arrived at Paris airport yesterday. It came from Spain.

____

c) The train is very fast. It leaves at 10 o'clock.

____

d) The house was sold. It has got more than ten rooms.

____

e) The neighbours moved to Birmingham. I like them very much.

____

Im schriftlichen Englisch findet man manchmal noch "whom" statt "who", wenn das Relativpronomen ein Objekt im Relativsatz ist.

The woman to whom the landlord gave 10 pounds was very poor.

Das Relativpronomen "whose"

Das Relativpronomen "whose" hat im Deutschen die Bedeutung von „dessen" und „deren". Meist bezieht es sich auf Personen, manchmal aber auch auf Dinge. Nach "whose" folgt immer ein Nomen.

This is the boy whose mother is my English teacher.
The doctor whose daughter is in my form is my father's friend.
The author whose book is a bestseller is my uncle.

Achte darauf, dass das Relativpronomen "whose" sehr leicht mit der Kurzform für "who is" = "who's" verwechselt werden kann.

This is my friend whose computer is broken.

Here comes the man who's repairing computers all day.

1 Überlege, ob in den Sätzen "whose" oder "who's" einzusetzen ist.

a) The man ____________ brother is a millionaire is still very poor.
b) Jim often plays with a boy ____________ parents are from Russia.
c) The boy ____________ my best friend has got six sisters.
d) The book ____________ cover is dirty is Bill's.
e) Mr Right is a teacher ____________ pupils like him very much.

2 Das sind Fotos von der Einschulung. Schreibe den Buchstaben des Satzes, der zum Bild passt, in den Kreis.

a) Mrs Brown is the woman whose son Tim has got a teddy.
b) Mrs Green is the woman whose daughter Judy has got a pink shirt.
c) Billy Black is the boy whose mother has got glasses.
d) Rose Grey is the girl whose mother has got a handbag.

3 Beantworte die Fragen:

a) Who's the boy whose mother has got a pink shirt?

____

b) Who's the woman whose daughter has got the biggest schoolbag?

____

Besonderheiten bei Relativsätzen

Immer dann, wenn das Relativpronomen das Objekt im Relativsatz ist, kann es im Englischen auch vollständig weggelassen werden. Die Bedeutung des Satzes bleibt dabei völlig gleich.

The TV show which we saw yesterday was very funny.	The TV show we saw yesterday was very funny.
The man who we met last night was a policeman.	The man we met last night was a policeman.

Manchmal ist ein Relativsatz zum näheren Verständnis des Satzes überhaupt nicht nötig. Das ist fast immer der Fall, wenn es sich um eine mit Namen benannte Person oder ein konkretes Ding handelt, auf das mit "this" oder "that" hingewiesen wird. In solchen Fällen wird der Relativsatz mit Kommas abgetrennt.

Mr Miller, who works at BBC Radio, has a nice daughter.
Keith, whose dog is named Bello, is 13 years old.

1 Nur bei zwei der folgenden Sätze kannst du das Relativpronomen weglassen. Kreuze sie an und schreibe sie dann ohne Relativpronomen auf.

a) We are proud of our Dad who has won the TV quiz.
b) The aunt who we'll visit next year lives in France.
c) The horse that won the race is very beautiful.
d) The homework which I'm doing now is very difficult.

____

____

____

2 Drei Sätze enthalten einen Relativsatz, der zum Verständnis nicht unbedingt nötig ist. Kreuze diese Sätze an und setze die Kommas richtig ein, die noch fehlen.

a) Kitty who has never been to Germany speaks German very well.
b) This coffee which is very hot looks very strange.
c) I met the teacher who you were talking about at the cinema.
d) The dog that Mr Brown gave me as a present is my favourite pet.
e) My Mum who doesn't like TV shows is working in the garden.

S. 4 1. five – one – six – two – four; two – four – nine – eight – six;
three – one – five – six – eight; four – two – eight – five – nine
2. six – o – o – nine – seven – three; one – nine – o – six – eight – nine;
three – o – eight – o – seven – five; eight – five – nine – eight – o – two
3. e) und h)

S. 5 1. 31, 63, 24, 84, 66, 59, 78
2. five, twelve, twenty-seven, forty-eight, fifty-five, one hundred

S. 6 1. b) four o'clock, c) twelve o'clock, d) one o'clock, e) eleven o'clock, f) two o'clock
2. a) six nineteen, b) five o seven, c) ten thirty-nine, d) o forty-one, e) three fifty-eight, f) seven o'clock, g) eleven thirty-two, h) eight thirteen, i) two twenty-one, j) twelve o'clock, k) four o seven

S. 7 1. a) five past eight, b) a quarter to six, c) ten past one, d) a quarter past twelve, e) half past four, f) nineteen minutes past four, g) thirteen minutes to ten, h) eighteen minutes past two, i) twelve minutes to nine

S. 8 1. 1st, 9th, 8th, 11th, 32nd, 44th, 50th, 15th, 61st, 83rd, 99th, 30th
2. third, seventh, first, fifty-sixth, ninety-ninth

S. 9 1. April, July, December, September, October, May, January, August, March, June, November, February
2. Monday, Tuesday, Wednesday, Thursday, Friday, Saturday, Sunday
3. Tuesday, Thursday, Saturday, Monday, Friday

S. 10 1. b) Mrs Miller / duck, c) Mr Smith / horse, d) Chris / dog e) Miss Clark / sheep, f) Susan / cat

S. 11 1. a) church, b) house, c) tower, d) plane, e) sun, f) bus, g) street, h) car, i) tree, j) ship, k) bridge, l) lorry
2. Streiche durch: a) flower, b) pencil, c) plane, d) bed, e) river

S. 12 1. b) the chair, c) the house, d) the tree, e) the flower, f) the moon, g) the table, h) the tower
2. b) a cat, c) a cow, d) a horse, e) a pig, f) a sheep, g) a bird, h) a duck

S. 13 1. a) a dog, b) an elephant, c) a cat, d) an ape; e) a sister, f) an uncle, g) a brother, h) an aunt, i) an orange, j) a banana, k) a tomato, l) an apple
2. b) an old man – a young man, c) a blue car – an orange car

S. 14 1. a) ears, b) eyes, c) lips, d) arms, e) hands, f) fingers, g) shoulders, h) legs, i) knees
2. Streiche durch: b) cup, c) plates, d) rabbits, e) rings, f) door, g) pillow, h) clouds

S. 15 1. a) boxes, b) buses, c) glasses, d) dresses
2. a) watches, b) brushes, c) dishes, d) churches
3. b) potatoes, c) tomatoes

S. 16 1. a) hobbies, b) families, c) parties, d) cities
2. b) boys, c) keys
3. a) lives, b) thieves, c) wives, d) shelves

S. 17 1. Plural mit -s: fingers, hands, dogs, cats; Plural und Singular gleich: sheep, fish, hair; unregelmäßiger Plural: teeth, men, feet, mice, women, children; Plural mit -ys nach Vokal: boys, toys, days, keys; Plural mit -es: boxes, watches, bushes, foxes; Plural mit -ies nach y und Konsonant: cities, families, parties, babies

S. 18 1. b) Laura's sister, c) Nick's car, d) father's son, e) Mary's horse, f) Ben's guitar
2. Richtig sind: d), a), d)

S. 19 1. a) the boys' books, b) the women's children, c) the girls' dolls, d) the teachers' pencils, e) the policemen's cars, f) the singers' song, g) the children's bikes
2. Richtig ist: c)

S. 20 1. a) the elephants of the zoo, b) the teachers of the school, c) the colours of the rainbow, d) the tower of the church, e) the name of the street, f) the brakes of the bike
2. Richtig sind: b) und g)

S. 21 1. a) the mouse of the computer, b) Jane's mouse, c) John's monkey, d) the monkeys of the zoo, e) Mr Baker's swimming pool, f) the swimming pool of the hotel
2. Richtig sind: a) und c)

S. 22 1. a) I am Kevin. b) You are my friend. c) He is my brother. She is my sister. It is his bike. d) We (They) are from Spain. e) You are very nice! f) They are very tired.

S. 23 1. Kreise ein: a) it, b) it, c) she, d) he, e) it, f) he
2. a) I am a girl. I am twelve. b) She is my sister. She is nice. c) He is a little child. He is two. d) They are teachers. e) We are a family. f) It is very old.

S. 25 1. Richtig sind: c), d), b), d)
2. a) I often play with him. b) Give it to them. c) My friend asks me what time it is. d) I like you. e) I will take it to her.

S. 26 1. a) This is her hamster. b) This is my new teacher. (Es könnte auch our oder your heißen.) c) This is our house. d) Can I have your book, please? e) The cat is in its basket. f) My friend and his sister.
2. Streiche durch: a) our, b) his, c) his, d) their

S. 27 1. Richtig sind: c), c), d)
2. a) my, b) our, c) his, d) its, e) mine f) ours

S. 28 1. a) to shout, b) to read, c) to drink, d) to cook, e) to swim, f) to sleep, g) to run, h) to eat
2. Streiche durch: a) to eat, b) to sleep, c) to drink

S. 29 1. a) doesn't, b) don't, c) doesn't, d) don't
2. b) She does her homework.

S. 30 1. a) He can't speak Spanish. b) Carmen can speak Spanish. She can't speak Turkish. c) Achmed can speak Turkish. He can't speak Russian. d) Irina can speak Russian. She can't speak French. e) Pierre can speak French. He can't speak Italian. f) Mario can speak Italian. He can't speak English.

S. 31 1. b) You're a nice girl. c) It isn't a dog. d) I'm not thirteen. e) He's a tall man. d) We aren't very hungry.

S. 32 1. b) We've got a cat. We haven't got a dog. c) They've got an apple. They haven't got a banana. d) I've got a cup. I haven't got a glass. e) She's got a skirt. She hasn't got a dress.

S. 33 1. a) He has a shower. b) We have a party. c) They have fun. d) She has a drink.
2. b) He has to check his computer. c) He has to visit his grandmother. d) He has to tidy up his room. e) He has to go to the doctor. f) He has to call his friend.

S. 34 1. a) I am (I'm) repairing my bike. b) You are (you're) watching TV. c) He is (he's) talking. d) They are (they're) playing football. e) You are (you're) singing together. f) We are (we're) reading a book.
2. Richtig sind: c), d), c)

S. 35 1. a) to swim, c) to ride, d) to stop, e) to begin, f) to make
2. a) sitting, b) shopping, c) giving, d) coming, e) lying, f) living

S. 36 1. b) We are not (aren't) playing cards. c) You are not (aren't) dancing. d) Mrs Bucks is not (isn't) coming. e) The women are not (aren't) shopping. f) She is not (isn't) singing. g) The bird is not (isn't) flying. h) Pete is not (isn't) riding his bike.
2. Richtig sind: d) und c)

S. 37 1. Richtig sind: a) und c)

S. 38 1. a) Linda eats. b) The baby sleeps. c) We swim. d) She drives. e) You work. f) My friends dance. g) I read. h) He paints.
2. a) go, b) smokes, c) go, d) drink, e) play

S. 39 1. a) First Sarah says goodbye to her mum. b) Then she takes her bike. c) After that she rides to school. d) Finally she enters the classroom.
2. a) First Ken awakes. b) Then he puts on his clothes. c) After that he has breakfast. d) Finally he brushes his teeth.

S. 40 1. b) I go to school. You don't go to school. c) I like tea. Mrs Smith doesn't like tea. d) We work in the garden. You don't work in the garden. e) Our cat likes milk. Our dog doesn't like milk. f) The children swim. Their parents don't swim. g) My father smokes. My mother doesn't smoke.
2. Richtig sind c) und c)

S. 41 1. a) gets up, b) is waiting, c) is reading, d) meets, e) sleeps, f) are singing, g) is brushing
2. a) I do not eat fish and chips. b) You aren't drinking water. c) He doesn't sleep at school. d) She doesn't drive a bus. e) He isn't doing the shopping.

S. 42 1. a) under, b) in front of, c) behind, d) on, e) over
2. Richtig sind: b), d) und d)

S. 43 1. a) in the picture, b) on the radio, c) in German, d) on TV, e) to go on foot, f) on the coast, g) on the phone, h) on the left, i) on the right, j) in the sky, k) in bed, l) on the train

S. 44 1. Die Sätze e), g) und h) passen nicht zum Bild.
2. a) into, b) in, c) into, d) into, e) in, f) in

S. 45 1. a) on, b) past, c) at, d) on, e) at
2. a) in winter, b) at night, c) at nine fifteen, d) on 24th December, e) on Sunday, f) at the end

S. 46 1. a) orange, b) yellow, c) green, d) blue, e) pink, f) brown, g) red, h) white, i) grey

2. Streiche durch: a) ugly, b) big, c) old, d) quick, e) quiet, f) sad

S. 47 1. b) a big green tree, c) a nice young girl, d) an old grey horse
2. b) The boy is tall. c) The music is loud. d) The horse is brown. e) The tomato is red.

S. 48 1. b) Bob sometimes plays tennis. c) I'm just reading a book.
2. a) never, b) usually, c) always, d) sometimes

S. 49 1. Adverbiale Bestimmungen des Ortes: at the hospital, in the country, on the train; adverbiale Bestimmungen der Zeit: every February, in summer, on Tuesday
2. a) Mum and Dad watch TV in the living room every evening. b) My grandparents never go to bed after midnight. c) I usually do my homework at the kitchen table from 4 until 5.

S. 50 1. b) Where is your school? c) How old is Tim? d) When are your parents at a party? e) Who can you see in the garden? f) What have we got?
2. a) where, b) what, c) when, d) why

S. 51 1. b) When do the stars shine? c) Where does our cat sit? d) Who does my mum help?
2. a) Who loves cats? b) Who does Kathy love? c) Who does Ken help? d) Who helps her mother?

S. 52 1. b) Do the children have fun? c) Is Patty Douglas' girlfriend? d) Does Dad read the newspaper every day? e) Do our guests leave at 5 o'clock? f) Can Keith come tomorrow? g) Is the dog barking?

2. b) Doesn't Mr Keiton often read books? c) Isn't the mobile phone ringing? d) Hasn't he got a new bike? e) Can't we do our homework later? f) Isn't Mrs Snuggs very busy today? g) Don't we usually go on holiday in July?

S. 53 1. a) Yes, he does. b) No, they aren't. c) No, we haven't. d) Yes, I do. oder: Yes, we do. e) No, she isn't. f) No, she can't.
2. a) Yes, I do. b) No, they aren't. c) Yes, he has. d) No, I can't.

S. 54 1. a) Lions, b) The birds, c) Dogs, cats, d) The flowers, e) milk, bananas
2. Richtig ist: d)

S. 55 1. a) much, b) many, c) much, d) many, e) many
2. a) much, b) a lot of, c) a lot of, d) lots of, e) much

S. 56 1. a) some, b) any, c) some, d) any, e) any
2. a) Bill has got some rubbers. Sarah hasn't got any rubbers. b) Bill hasn't got any biros. Sarah has got some biros. c) Bill has got some cookies. Sarah hasn't got any cookies. d) Bill hasn't got any chocolate. Sarah has got some chocolate. e) Bill doesn't drink any milk. Sarah usually drinks some milk.

S. 57 1. a) any, b) some, c) any, d) any, e) some, f) any

S. 58 1. b) The girl is young. She's a young girl. c) The noise is terrible. It's a terrible noise. d) The children are happy. They are happy children. e) The woman is beautiful. She's a beautiful woman. f) The sky is blue. It's a blue sky.
2. Unterstreiche: a) hungry, b) lazy, old, c) funny, d) ----, e) new

S. 59 1. Richtig sind: d/g, b/f, c/h, a/e

S. 60 1. b) younger, youngest, c) faster, fastest, d) deeper, deepest, e) taller, tallest, f) cheaper, cheapest, g) brighter, brightest, h) warmer, warmest
2. a) long, b) longer, c) longest

S. 61 1. a) nicer, nicest, b) happier, happiest, c) hotter, hottest, d) dirtier, dirtiest, e) smaller, smallest, f) angrier, angriest, g) heavier, heaviest, h) funnier, funniest
2. a) hot, b) hotter, c) hottest

S. 62 1. Unterstreiche: expensive, tired, aggressive, exciting, careful, boring, marvellous, terrible, difficult
2. a) expensive, more expensive, most expensive, b) tired, more tired, most tired, c) aggressive, more aggressive, most aggressive, d) exciting, more exciting, most exciting, e) careful, more careful, most careful, f) boring, more boring, most boring, g) marvellous, more marvellous, most marvellous, h) terrible, more terrible, most terrible i) difficult, more difficult, most difficult
3. a) most intelligent, b) most terrible, c) most expensive

S. 63 1. sweet, sweeter, sweetest; happy, happier, happiest; difficult, more difficult, most difficult; beautiful, more beautiful, most beautiful
2. a) taller, tallest, b) sillier, silliest, c) more marvellous, most marvellous, d) newer, newest, e) more nervous, most nervous, f) greater, greatest, g) higher, highest, h) happier, happiest

S. 64 1. b) Ann's hair is longer than Tom's hair. c) Tom's hair is darker than Ann's hair. d) Tom's bag is bigger than Ann's bag. e) Ann's bag is smaller than Tom's bag.
2. b) I'm older than her. c) I'm as funny as him. d) The Smiths are as rich as us. e) My brother is younger than me.

S. 65 1. b) My hair is not as long as Mary's hair. c) I'm less beautiful than Mary. d) My legs are not as slim as Mary's legs. e) I'm less intelligent than Mary. f) I'm not as funny as Mary. g) My voice is less fantastic than Mary's voice. h) My eyes are not as bright as Mary's eyes. i) I'm less attractive than Mary.
2. a) The trousers are more expensive than the hat. b) The hat is as cheap as the shirt. c) The socks are cheaper than the hat. d) The shirt is less expensive than the trousers (oder: not as expensive as). e) The shirt is as expensive as the hat. f) The hat is cheaper than the trousers.

S. 66 1. a) carefully, b) loudly, c) greatly, d) badly, e) nervously, f) tenderly
2. a) quick, b) quickly, c) dangerous, d) dangerously, e) brightly, f) bright

S. 67 1. a) easily, b) fantastically, c) early, d) prettily, e) well, f) electronically, g) terribly, h) daily, i) hard, j) long
2. a) Adverb, b) Adjektiv, c) Adjektiv, d) Adverb

S. 68 1. b) Dad shouts angrily. Grandpa shouts more angrily. Mum shouts most angrily. c) Kim sings terribly. Mary sings more terribly. Ronald sings most terribly. d) Cindy plays the guitar well. Dave plays the guitar better. Brian plays the guitar best. e) Fred does his homework badly. Frank does his homework worse. John does his homework worst.

S. 69 1. b) The earthworm runs faster than the snail. c) The spider runs as fast as the ant. d) The snail doesn't run as fast as the caterpillar. e) The earthworm doesn't run as fast as the ant. f) The caterpillar runs as fast as the earthworm.
2. b) The earthworm crawls as slowly as the caterpillar. c) The earthworm crawls more slowly than the spider. d) The spider crawls as slowly as the ant. e) The earthworm crawls less slowly than the snail. f) The spider crawls less slowly than the snail.

S. 70 1. a) he runs, b) Sam laughs, c) we whisper, d) it shines, e) they phone, f) you wait
2. a) hates, b) sleep, c) loves, d) sing, e) waits

S. 71 1. b) we are / we're, c) it is / it's, d) you have / you've, e) they have / they've, f) she has / she's
2. b) he hasn't, c) we aren't, d) it doesn't, e) they haven't, f) she isn't

S. 72 1. a) The cat is sleeping. b) Mary is singing. c) You are jumping. d) The football players are shouting. e) We are working in the garden. f) I am doing my homework.
2. a) making, b) putting, c) listening, d) writing, e) running, f) raining, g) dancing, h) shopping, i) going, j) swimming

S. 73 1. a) I am listening to the radio. b) It usually rains in Scotland. c) Danny is writing a letter to his Dad now. d) Mrs Diver always does the shopping on Friday.
e) Look, the man over there is dancing in the street.
2. Richtig sind: We usually play tennis on Saturday. Alice is doing the shopping now.

S. 74 1. b) You don't read newspapers. c) Our cat doesn't sleep in its basket. d) My sister doesn't like ice cream. e) My father doesn't play the piano. f) Their parents don't play chess.
2. b) Adults usually don't go to school. c) Fred can't go to school by bus. d) The Millers haven't got a TV. e) You don't often go to the theatre. f) You don't like your teachers.

S. 75 1. a) where, b) how, c) what, d) who, e) why
2. b) Is Debbie's pencil blue? c) Does John play football every Monday? d) Can we go to the zoo on Sunday?

S. 76 1. a) Simon is going to play computer games. b) The children are going to buy tickets.
c) The dog is going to catch a cat. d) We are going to buy a new car.
2. b) I'm not going to have English lessons. d) David isn't going to eat ice cream.

S. 77 1. b) Who is going to drink milk? c) Where is Mr Green going to go? d) When is my uncle going to come? e) What is the plane going to do? f) Who am I going to meet?
2. b) No, we aren't. c) Yes, they are. d) Yes, I am. e) No, it isn't. f) No, I'm not.

S. 78 1. b) She'll have a baby in May. c) They'll move to London. d) It'll shine tomorrow.
2. b) I think England will win the football championship next time.
c) I'm sure we'll have fun at the party.

S. 79 1. b) Ann won't enjoy your party. c) You won't go to McDonald's.
d) Our neighbours won't watch TV.
2. a) When will it rain? b) What will you sell? c) When will our aunt visit us?
d) Who will sing a song on my birthday?

S. 80 1. b) The boat is leaving for New York on Monday. c) We are listening to the radio tomorrow. d) My parents are flying to London this afternoon.
2. Verlaufsform der Gegenwart: a) We're going to the theatre next Friday.
b) My uncle is coming this afternoon. Going-to-Futur: a) I'm going to feed my dog.
b) The plane is going to take off in one minute.

S. 81 1. a) We are going to watch the new film. b) Maybe it will be nice weather tomorrow.
c) I think you will win the tennis match next Sunday. d) My sister is going to make a cake. e) I'm sure Grandpa will work this afternoon.
2. Trage ein: a), b)

S. 82 1. a) I answered. Nick answered. You answered. b) You walked. She walked. The girls walked. c) Kate shouted. We shouted. You shouted. d) He listened. We listened. They listened. e) You worked. She worked. The men worked. f) Ken opened. He opened. You opened.
2. a) We climbed up a tree. b) We walked into a cave. c) We played tennis.

S. 83 1. a) arrived, b) visited, c) moved, d) planned, e) stopped, f) tried
2. Richtig ist: d) Sally is watching TV now.

S. 84 1. a) took, b) sold, c) went, d) bought, e) met, f) did, g) had, h) ate, i) made

S. 85 1. a) were, b) was, c) were, d) were
2. b) Was Henry at the cinema yesterday? No, he wasn't. c) Were you in Denmark last summer? Yes, we were. d) Were you on the sports field last week? No, I wasn't.

S. 86 1. b) Kevin didn't collect eggs. c) The children didn't make hay. d) Greg didn't water the vegetables. e) The girls didn't feed the pigs. f) The boys didn't pick apples. g) Tom didn't repair the tractor.

S. 87 1. a) No, he didn't. b) Yes, we did. c) Yes, I did. d) No, she didn't.
2. a) slept, b) won, c) sat, d) heard, e) caught, f) went

S. 88 1. b) You were running. c) Cedric was coming. d) We were shouting. e) They were listening. f) She was going.
2. Richtig ist: c)

S. 89 1. b) Sarah wasn't playing computer games. c) Keith wasn't reading a book. d) The twins weren't painting a picture. e) Grandpa wasn't sleeping. f) Grandma wasn't smoking a pipe. g) The dogs weren't eating chocolate.
2. a) Yes, they were. b) No, we weren't. c) No, he wasn't. d) Yes, I was.

S. 90 1. a) I have washed. b) You have cleaned. c) He has visited. d) We have walked. e) They have painted. f) You have tried. g) It has rested. h) She has laughed.
2. b), c), a)

S. 91 1. a) I have just watched a bank robbery. b) The thieves have run away. c) They have stolen a lot of money. d) They have frightened a lot of people.
2. a) He has listened. b) We have broken. c) They have worked. d) You have paid. e) She has gone. f) I have taken. g) You have written. h) We have eaten.

S. 92 1. b) Daniel hasn't done his homework yet. c) Dave hasn't fed his rabbit yet. d) Mary hasn't cleaned her room yet. e) Jane hasn't done the shopping yet.
2. a) No, we haven't. b) Yes, he has. c) No, I haven't. d) Yes, we have. e) Yes, she has.

S. 93 1. a) I visited my grandparents last year. b) We have had breakfast just now. c) My father had an accident last summer. d) He went into the library last week. e) She found her pencil an hour ago.
2. Richtig sind: a), d), e)

S. 94 1. a) skiing, b) swimming, c) fishing, d) boxing, e) running, f) jumping
2. In den Sätzen a), b) und f) kommt ein Gerundium vor.

S. 95 1. a) No fishing! b) Dancing club c) No smoking!
2. a) Schwimmen macht Spaß. b) Auf den Bus zu warten macht mich wütend. c) Singen ist Sallys Hobby. d) Nach Hause zu kommen ist immer toll.

S. 96 1. a) Dad avoided getting wet. b) Willy missed playing computer games. c) Mary liked playing with other children. d) Mum risked getting sunburn.
2. Satz c) 3. Richtig ist: b)

S. 97 1. a) Dennis is looking forward to having a party. b) Dad is interested in repairing old clocks. c) Patty is dreaming of being a piano player. d) Tanja is proud of having many friends. e) Bob is crazy about playing computer games. f) Pia is crazy about meeting her boyfriend.

S. 98 1. a) who, b) what, c) I, d) the children, e) Dad, f) Sally, g) who, h) what
2. a) David, b) David, Kevin, c) Kevin, David, d) the dog, e) barking, f) David

S. 99 1. b) Ann's. Hers. c) Kitty's. Hers. d) Mitch's. His. e) Bello's. His. f) Ben's. His.
2. a) what, b) which, c) what, d) who, e) which, f) which, g) which

S. 100 1. a) ... hasn't he? b) ... can't you? c) ... isn't she? d) ... has he? e) ... is she? f) ... can you?

2. a) ... aren't they? b) ... can he? c) ... isn't she? d) ... hasn't it? e) ... is she? f) ... do they? g) ... can we?

S. 101 1. a) ... does he? b) ... didn't it? c) ... don't they? d) ... doesn't he? e) ... didn't she? f) ... doesn't it?
2. a) ... will she? b) ... didn't we? c) ... isn't it? d) ... don't they? e) ... don't I? f) aren't they?

S. 102 1. a) because, b) but, c) that, d) before, e) after, f) until
2. b), a), c), e), f), d)

S. 103 1. a) Dave spent a lot of time in hospital when he was a little boy. b) The weather was really nice so we had lots of fun in the swimming pool. c) You can't learn English words while you are listening to the radio. d) The plane made a terrible noise as it took off from the airport.
2. a) because, b) but, c) when, d) that, e) so, f) until

S. 104 1. a) If Emma meets Tim today, she'll be very happy. b) We'll go to the cinema if Mum gives us some money. c) If I win a hundred pounds, I'll buy a new bike. d) Dad will get mad if you don't stop this music. e) If Bill comes to the disco, he'll see his old friends. f) The Taylors will go to the theatre if they get a babysitter.
2. a), c), e)
3. d), f), a)

S. 105 1. a) when, b) if, c) if, d) when
2. b) If we are early, we will get a good place in the cinema. c) The children will invite many friends if the parents are not at home. d) If Dad comes home before 5 o'clock, he will try to repair my bike. e) Mr Smith will help us if we do his shopping this week.

S. 106 1. a) which, b) who, c) which, d) who, e) which, f) who
2. a) Phil, b) Marion, c) Tibs, d) Hugh, e) Ella, f) Banjee

S. 107 1. Subjektstellung: Sätze b) und c), Objektstellung: Sätze a), d)
2. a) The plane which came from Spain arrived at Paris airport yesterday. b) The train which leaves at 10 o'clock is very fast. c) The house which has got more than ten rooms was sold. d) The neighbours who I like very much moved to Birmingham.

S. 108 1. a) whose, b) whose, c) who's, d) whose, e) whose
2. c), a), b), d)
3. a) It's Tim. b) It's Mrs Grey.

S. 109 1. The aunt we'll visit next year lives in France. The homework I'm doing now is very difficult.
2. a) Kitty, who has never been to Germany, speaks German very well. b) This coffee, which is very hot, looks very strange. e) My Mum, who doesn't like TV shows, is working in the garden.

Infinitiv	Imperfekt	Partizip	deutscher Infinitiv
to be	was	been	sein
to become	became	become	werden
to begin	began	begun	beginnen
to bite	bit	bitten	beißen
to blow	blew	blown	wehen, blasen
to break	broke	broken	brechen, zerbrechen, kaputtgehen
to bring	brought	brought	bringen
to build	built	built	bauen
to burn	burnt (burned)	burnt (burned)	brennen
to buy	bought	bought	kaufen
to catch	caught	caught	fangen
to choose	chose	chosen	wählen, auswählen, aussuchen
to come	came	come	kommen
to cost	cost	cost	kosten
to cut	cut	cut	schneiden, ausschneiden
to do	did	done	tun, machen
to draw	drew	drawn	zeichnen
to drink	drank	drunk	trinken
to drive	drove	driven	fahren (Auto, Bus, Traktor usw.)
to eat	ate	eaten	essen
to fall	fell	fallen	fallen, hinfallen
to feed	fed	fed	füttern
to feel	felt	felt	fühlen, sich fühlen
to find	found	found	finden
to fly	flew	flown	fliegen
to forget	forgot	forgotten	vergessen
to get	got	got	bekommen, holen, besorgen, gelangen, hinkommen, werden
to give	gave	given	geben
to go	went	gone	gehen
to grow	grew	grown	wachsen
to have	had	had	haben, besitzen (have got)
to hear	heard	heard	hören
to hide	hid	hidden	verstecken
to hit	hit	hit	schlagen
to hold	held	held	halten, festhalten
to hurt	hurt	hurt	verletzen
to keep	kept	kept	halten, behalten
to know	knew	known	wissen, kennen

Infinitiv	Imperfekt	Partizip	deutscher Infinitiv
to lay	laid	lain	legen
to lead	led	led	führen
to learn	learnt	learnt	lernen
to leave	left	left	verlassen, weggehen, abfahren
to lend	lent	lent	leihen, verleihen
to let	let	let	lassen
to lie	lay	lain	liegen
to lose	lost	lost	verlieren
to make	made	made	machen
to mean	meant	meant	meinen, bedeuten
to meet	met	met	treffen, sich treffen
to overtake	overtook	overtaken	überholen
to pay	paid	paid	bezahlen
to put	put	put	legen, stellen
to read	read	read	lesen
to ride	rode	ridden	reiten; to ride a bike = Fahrrad fahren
to ring	rang	rung	klingeln, läuten
to say	said	said	sagen, sprechen
to see	saw	seen	sehen
to seek	sought	sought	suchen
to sell	sold	sold	verkaufen
to send	sent	sent	schicken, senden, absenden
to shake	shook	shaken	schütteln, zittern
to show	showed	shown	zeigen
to shut	shut	shut	schließen, abschließen
to sing	sang	sung	singen
to sink	sank	sunk	sinken, untergehen
to sit	sat	sat	sitzen
to sleep	slept	slept	schlafen
to speak	spoke	spoken	sprechen
to spend	spent	spent	verbringen
to stand	stood	stood	stehen
to steal	stole	stolen	stehlen
to swim	swam	swum	schwimmen
to take	took	taken	nehmen
to tell	told	told	erzählen
to think	thought	thought	denken
to throw	threw	thrown	werfen
to understand	understood	understood	verstehen
to win	won	won	gewinnen
to write	wrote	written	schreiben

a	ein / eine
a lot of / lots of	viel / eine Menge
accident	Unfall
across	über
to admit	zugeben
adult	Erwachsener
after	nach
afternoon	Nachmittag
aggressive	aggressiv
airport	Flughafen
alarm	Alarm
almost	fast
already	schon
always	immer
an hour ago	vor einer Stunde
angry	wütend, ärgerlich
animal	Tier
answer	Antwort
to answer	antworten
ant	Ameise
any	irgendein / irgendeine
ape	Menschenaffe
apple	Apfel
April	April
arm	Arm
around	um ... herum
to arrive	ankommen
as	als, während
to ask	fragen
at home	zu Hause
attractive	attraktiv
August	August
aunt	Tante
author	Autor
automatic	automatisch
autumn	Herbst
to avoid	vermeiden
to awake	aufwachen
away	weg, fort
awful	schrecklich
baby	Baby
back	zurück
bad	schlecht
ball	Ball
banana	Banane
bank robbery	Banküberfall
to bark	bellen
basket	Korb
bath	Bad
to be	sein
to be able to	können, in der Lage sein
to be afraid of	vor etwas Angst haben
to be interested in	an etwas Interesse haben
to be lucky	Glück haben
to be pleased	sich über etw. freuen
beach	Strand
beautiful	schön
because	weil
bed	Bett
bedroom	Schlafzimmer
beer	Bier
before	vor, vorher, bevor
to begin	beginnen, anfangen
behind	hinter
to believe	glauben
big	groß
bike	Fahrrad
bird	Vogel
birthday	Geburtstag
black	schwarz
blue	blau
boat	Boot
book	Buch
boring	langweilig
box	Schachtel, Kiste, Karton
to box	boxen
boy	Junge
brakes	Bremsen
bread	Brot
to break	brechen, zerbrechen
breakfast	Frühstück
bridge	Brücke
bright	hell
brother	Bruder
brown	braun
brush	Bürste
to brush	bürsten
bus	Bus
bus stop	Bushaltestelle
busy	beschäftigt
but	aber
to buy	kaufen
cage	Käfig
cake	Kuchen

to call	anrufen, rufen
can	können
car	Auto
to care for	sich kümmern
careful	vorsichtig
to carry	tragen
cat	Katze
to catch	fangen
caterpillar	Raupe
cave	Höhle
century	Jahrhundert
chair	Stuhl
championship	Meisterschaft
cheap	billig
to check	überprüfen
cheese	Käse
chess	Schach
child	Kind
chocolate	Schokolade
Christmas	Weihnachten
church	Kirche
cinema	Kino
circus	Zirkus
city	Stadt, Innenstadt
classroom	Klassenzimmer
to clean	putzen, reinigen
to climb	klettern
clock	Uhr
clothes	Kleidung
cloud	Wolke
clown	Clown
coach	Trainer
coast	Küste
coat	Mantel
coffee	Kaffee
cold	kalt
to collect	sammeln
Cologne	Köln
colour	Farbe
to come	kommen
to cook	kochen
to cost	kosten
to count	zählen
country	Land
cow	Kuh
to crawl	krabbeln
crazy	verrückt
crocodile	Krokodil
to crowd	sich drängen
to cry	weinen, schreien
cup	Tasse
cupboard	Schrank
curtain	Vorhang
to cycle	Rad fahren
daily	täglich
to dance	tanzen
dangerous	gefährlich
dark	dunkel
date	Datum
daughter	Tochter
day	Tag
December	Dezember
deep	tief
Denmark	Dänemark
difficult	schwierig
dinner	Abendessen
dirty	schmutzig
dishes	Geschirr
to do	tun, machen
doctor	Arzt
dog	Hund
door	Tür
down	unten, hinunter
to draw	zeichnen
to dream	träumen
dress	Kleid
to drink	trinken
to drive	fahren
driver	Fahrer
to drop	fallen lassen
drunken	betrunken
duck	Ente
ear	Ohr
early	früh
earthworm	Regenwurm
easy	einfach
to eat	essen
egg	Ei
electronic	elektronisch
elephant	Elefant
to endanger	gefährden
English	englisch, Englisch
to enjoy	genießen
enough	genug
to enter	betreten
evening	Abend
every	jeder, jede, jedes
exciting	aufregend

expensive	teuer
eye	Auge
to fall	fallen
family	Familie
famous	berühmt
fantastic	fantastisch
far	weit, fern
farmer	Bauer
fast	schnell
father	Vater
favourite food	Lieblingsessen
February	Februar
to feed	füttern
fence	Zaun
few	einige, ein paar
film	Film
finally	schließlich
fine	fein, gut
finger	Finger
first	zuerst, erstens
fish	Fisch
to fish	fischen, angeln
floor	Fußboden
flower	Blume
to fly	fliegen
foot	Fuß
football	Fußball
football match	Fußballspiel
football players	Fußballspieler
for	für
form / class	Klasse
France	Frankreich
French	französisch
Friday	Freitag
friend	Freund / Freundin
to frighten s.o.	jem. Angst machen
from	von, aus
fun	Spaß
funny	lustig, witzig
game	Spiel
garden	Garten
German	deutsch, Deutsch
Germany	Deutschland
to get	bekommen
to get up	aufstehen
girl	Mädchen
to give	geben
to give up	aufgeben
glass	Glas

glasses	Brille
to go	gehen
to go on	weitermachen
good	gut
goodbye	Auf Wiedersehen
grandparents	Großeltern
great	großartig
Great Britain	Großbritannien
green	grün
grey	grau
guest	Gast
guitar	Gitarre
hair	Haar
hamster	Hamster
hand	Hand
handbag	Handtasche
happy	glücklich
hard	hart
hardly	kaum
to hate	hassen
to have	haben
to have a bath	baden
to have a shower	duschen
to have fun	Spaß haben
hay	Heu
head	Kopf
health	Gesundheit
to hear	hören
heavy	schwer
to help	helfen
hen	Henne
hero	Held
high	hoch
hobby	Hobby
holiday(s)	Ferien, Urlaub
homework	Hausaufgaben
horrible	grauenhaft
horse	Pferd
hospital	Krankenhaus
hot	heiß
hour	Stunde
house	Haus
how	wie
hungry	hungrig
ice cream	Eis, Eiscreme
ill	krank
to imagine	sich etwas vorstellen
in	in
in front of	vor (örtlich)

in time	rechtzeitig
intelligent	intelligent
interesting	interessant
into	hinein
to invite	einladen
Ireland	Irland
island	Insel
Italian	italienisch
Italy	Italien
January	Januar
journey	Reise
July	Juli
to jump	springen
June	Juni
just	gerade
key	Schlüssel
kitchen	Küche
knee	Knie
to knock	klopfen, anklopfen
lady	Dame
late	spät
to laugh	lachen
lazy	faul
to learn	lernen
to leave	verlassen
left	links
leg	Bein
lemon juice	Zitronensaft
less	weniger
lesson	Lektion, Schulstunde
letter	Brief
library	Bibliothek, Bücherei
to lie	liegen; auch: lügen
life	Leben
to like	mögen
lion	Löwe
lip	Lippe
to listen	zuhören
little	klein
to live	leben, wohnen
living room	Wohnzimmer
long	lang
to look for	suchen
to look forward to	sich auf etwas freuen
lorry	Lastwagen
lots of / a lot of	viel / eine Menge
loud	laut
to love	lieben
lunch	Mittagessen

to make	machen
man	Mann, Mensch
many	viele
March	März
to marry	heiraten
marvellous	wunderbar
may	dürfen
May	Mai
maybe	möglicherweise
meat	Fleisch
medicine	Medizin
to meet	treffen
midnight	Mitternacht
milk	Milch
to milk	melken
minute	Minute
to miss	vermissen, verpassen
mobile phone	Handy
moment	Moment
Monday	Montag
money	Geld
monkey	Affe
monster	Monster
month	Monat
moon	Mond
more	mehr
morning	Morgen
most	am meisten
mother	Mutter
mouse	Maus
to move	bewegen, umzichen
much	viel
music	Musik
must	müssen
must not	nicht dürfen
name / last name	Name / Nachname
neighbour	Nachbar
nervous	nervös
never	niemals
new	neu
newspaper	Zeitung
next year	nächstes Jahr
nice	nett, schön
night	Nacht
noise	Geräusch
noisy	geräuschvoll, laut
nose	Nase
November	November

now	jetzt
October	Oktober
often	oft
old	alt
on	auf
on foot	zu Fuß
onto	hinauf
to open	öffnen
orange	orange
out of	hinaus
outside	draußen
over	über
over there	dort drüben
owl	Eule
to paint	malen
parents	Eltern
to park	parken
parrot	Papagei
party	Party, Fest
to pay	bezahlen
pen	Füller
pencil	Bleistift
pencil case	Federmappe
people	Leute
pepper	Pfeffer
person	Person
pet	Haustier
phone	Telefon
to phone	telefonieren
photo	Foto
piano	Klavier
to pick up	etwas aufheben
picture	Bild
pig	Schwein
pillow	Kopfkissen
pink	rosa
pipe	Pfeife
place	Platz, Ort
to plan	planen
plane	Flugzeug
plate	Teller
to play	spielen
please	bitte
pocket	Tasche
police	Polizei
policeman	Polizist
pond	Teich
poor	arm
port	Hafen

postcard	Postkarte
potato	Kartoffel
pound	Pfund
to practise	üben
to prefer	vorziehen, bevorzugen
present	Geschenk
president	Präsident
pretty	hübsch
proud	stolz
pupil	Schüler
to put	setzen, stellen, legen
question	Frage
quick	schnell
quiet	leise, ruhig
quite	ziemlich
rabbit	Kaninchen
race	Rennen
radio	Radio
railway station	Bahnhof
rain	Regen
to rain	regnen
rainbow	Regenbogen
rarely	selten
to read	lesen
really	wirklich
record	Schallplatte
red	rot
relatives	Verwandte
to rent	mieten
to repair	reparieren
to rest	ausruhen
restaurant	Restaurant
to retire	sich zur Ruhe setzen
rich	reich
to ride	fahren, reiten
right	richtig, rechts
to ring	klingeln, läuten
to risk	riskieren
river	Fluss
room	Zimmer
rose	Rose
rubber	Radiergummi
to run	rennen
Russia	Russland
Russian	russisch, Russisch
sad	traurig
salad	Salat
Saturday	Samstag

to say	sagen
school	Schule
schoolbag	Schultasche
Scotland	Schottland
to see	sehen
seldom	selten
to sell	verkaufen
September	September
shall	sollen
sheep	Schaf
shelf	Regal
to shine	scheinen
ship	Schiff
shirt	Hemd
shoe	Schuh
shop	Geschäft
to shop	einkaufen
short	kurz
shoulder	Schulter
to shout	rufen
to show	zeigen
shower	Dusche
shrimps	Krabben
to shut	schließen
sick	unwohl, krank
silly	dumm
to sing	singen
sister	Schwester
to sit	sitzen
skirt	Rock
sky	Himmel
to sleep	schlafen
slim	schlank
slow	langsam
small	klein
to smell	riechen
to smoke	rauchen
snail	Schnecke
so	deshalb, daher, also
some	manche, einige, einiges
someone	jemand
something	etwas
sometimes	manchmal
somewhere	irgendwo
son	Sohn
song	Lied
soon	bald
Spain	Spanien
Spanish	spanisch
to speak	sprechen
to spend	verbringen
spider	Spinne
sports field	Sportplatz
spring	Frühling
stadium	Stadion
stamps	Briefmarken
star	Stern
to start	starten, anfangen
to stay	bleiben
to steal	stehlen
still	immer noch
to stop	aufhören, anhalten
strange	fremd
street	Straße
sugar	Zucker
to suggest	vorschlagen
summer	Sommer
sun	Sonne
Sunday	Sonntag
supermarket	Supermarkt
supper	Abendessen
to suppose	annehmen
sure	sicher
swan	Schwan
Sweden	Schweden
sweet	süß
to swim	schwimmen
swimming pool	Schwimmbecken
table	Tisch
to take	nehmen
to take off	abheben, starten
to take place	stattfinden
to talk	reden
tall	groß
tea	Tee
teacher	Lehrer
telephone	Telefon
tender	zärtlich
tennis	Tennis
terrible	furchtbar, schrecklich
than	als
thank you	danke
theatre	Theater
then	dann
thief	Dieb
to think	denken

through	durch
Thursday	Donnerstag
ticket	Eintrittskarte, Fahrkarte
to tidy up	aufräumen
tiger	Tiger
time	Zeit
tiny	winzig
tired	müde
today	heute
together	zusammen
tomato	Tomate
tomorrow	morgen
tonight	heute Abend, heute Nacht
tooth	Zahn
tower	Turm
toy	Spielzeug
tractor	Traktor
traffic lights	Ampel
train	Zug
tree	Baum
trousers	Hose
to try	versuchen
Tuesday	Dienstag
Turkish	türkisch
twins	Zwillinge
ugly	hässlich
umbrella	Regenschirm
uncle	Onkel
under	unter
to understand	verstehen
uniform	Uniform
United States	Vereinigte Staaten
until	bis
to use	gebrauchen, benutzen
usually	gewöhnlich, normalerweise
vegetable	Gemüse
very	sehr
to visit	besuchen
visitor	Besucher
to wait	warten
to walk	gehen, spazieren gehen
wall	Wand
to want to	wollen
warm	warm
to wash	waschen
watch	Armbanduhr
to watch	beobachten, schauen
to water	gießen
way	Weg
to wear	tragen (Kleidung)
weather	Wetter
Wednesday	Mittwoch
week	Woche
weekend	Wochenende
weekly	wöchentlich
Welcome!	Willkommen!
wet	nass
what	was
wheel	Rad
when	wenn, als, wann
where	wo, wohin
which	welche, welcher, welches
while	während
to whisper	flüstern
white	weiß
who	wer, wen
whole	ganz
whose	wessen
why	warum
wife	Ehefrau
wild	wild
to win	gewinnen
window	Fenster
winner	Gewinner
winter	Winter
with	mit
woman	Frau
wood	Wald
words	Wörter
to work	arbeiten
world	Welt
worm	Wurm
to worry	sich sorgen
to write	schreiben
yellow	gelb
yesterday	gestern
yet	schon / noch nicht
young	jung
youth club	Jugendklub
zoo	Zoo